HOW
TO GET
A JOB

HAMLYN HELP YOURSELF GUIDE

HOW TO GET A JOB

BILL LUBBOCK
AND
RICHARD STOKES

HAMLYN

First published in 1989 by
The Hamlyn Publishing Group Limited,
a division of the Octopus Publishing Group,
Michelin House, 81 Fulham Road,
London SW3 6RB

ISBN 0 600 56627 7

Printed and bound by The Guernsey Press

Contents

1

Organise Yourself

This guide should help you to improve your chances of obtaining a job in competition with other candidates. By adopting the practical recommendations you will be able to make a stronger impact on paper and present yourself more effectively at subsequent interviews. Furthermore, you will learn how to explore the hidden job market and discover some of those attractive appointments which are never advertised.

This book has been prepared for four broad categories of reader:

- Leavers from schools or colleges seeking employment for the first time.
- People who have been dismissed, declared redundant, or invited to resign;
- Those in work who have become bored, frustrated, or under-utilised and seek a change;
- The ambitious whose career progression is blocked and need to move to achieve greater responsibility and higher pay.

Personnel advisers, career counsellors, and educationalists may also find this guide useful.

Many people have never analysed the job search process systematically – perhaps because some years have elapsed since they last sought employment; or because 'the job came to them' during a period of low unemployment and keen competition for staff; or because they are applying for a job for the first time.

This book will take you through the job search process step by step and enable you to polish your performance. Of course no one can create employment opportunities where they do not exist. Nevertheless, even in areas of high unemployment, it is well worth organising and launching a determined attack on the job market to ensure that you will be considered for the relatively few opportunities which will occur.

The entire job search process constitutes an exercise in self-marketing. It is really a matter of regarding yourself as a product to be sold. As a human being you possess some unique qualities. Those distinctive assets must be identified and then presented skilfully to your chosen market.

Systematic job seeking is not simply responding to vacancy advertisements. The process must be creative rather than reactive. You must sell yourself by persuading a company that the organisation would benefit from employing you and utilising your abilities. If you are out of a job, you will have to work as hard at finding another job as you would be working when in employment.

Once you have decided to embark on a job search, you must organise yourself properly. There are six golden rules to remember:-

Rule 1 – Prepare a job search action plan

Decide how much time you intend to devote to the job search as a minimum. Eight hours a day, five days a week perhaps, if you are unemployed?

Then you need to log the time which you actually do spend seeking employment. A few sheets of paper ruled vertically into seven columns, one for each day of the week, with times listed at the side in 30 minute intervals, will enable you to keep track of your efforts. Temporary work for, say, up to two days a week, can provide a useful break from job-hunting, especially if the work is in a field related to your normal employment. You will be able to extend your range of contacts and keep up to date in your field. Beware of the temptation to be sidetracked. Do not allow your temporary arrangements to detract from your over-riding goal – the pursuit of that ideal job.

Transfer your mental commitment to a visual aid. A poster-size board in the kitchen and/or bathroom is ideal. You will then be able to monitor your performance regularly. There is nothing wrong in spending the occasional half-day, or even full day, on a social event – provided that you compensate by equivalent overtime later. The board also will serve as a constant reminder of your main objective – finding the right job.

Rule 2 – Do not allow yourself to be diverted

Other people may assume that you have time on your hands,

especially if you are unemployed. Much as you may love your wife, husband, or partner, the temptation to redecorate the bedroom, improve the garden, or undertake a hundred small tasks around the house must be resisted. 'Passing away the time' is a luxury which you cannot afford. Once your self-marketing campaign has been launched successfully, you can begin to consider the occasional short break or diversion as a treat.

Rule 3 – Provide yourself with office equipment

As a minimum you will require some black ballpoint pens; good quality white A4 paper, with matching envelopes; a ringbinder and punch; three card index boxes; and scrap paper or notepads.

Always write using black biro, ink or rollerball. If your letter or career history is interesting enough, it may be photocopied by a prospective employer and circulated to several executives. Blue and other coloured inks do not photocopy as successfully as black inks. Any recipient of a poor photocopy may assume that you forwarded the original document in similar unimpressive form.

The other equipment is essential to enable you to keep track of all the letters which you will forward and all the replies which you will receive. By the time you have concluded your self-marketing campaign successfully, you may have written over 200 letters and attended 20 or more interviews in order to obtain an offer of a job which you are keen to accept.

Some people may need to make more applications – others less. The number will depend on many factors, including your age, employment history, qualifications, health, salary level, and the geographical area within which you are seeking a job. Regrettably, illegal discrimination, (particularly race discrimination and sex discrimination) can reduce your employment prospects severely. (Chapter 10 looks at this unfortunate and serious problem).

Rule 4 – Find yourself a 'workstation'

You will need a study, spare room, or underused room that you can commandeer for conversion into a job-search workstation. For those in a one or two-bedroom flat, space may be at a premium. With ingenuity even the overcrowded job hunter can find a small area which can be transformed into a workstation. You will need to operate from a base which will not be in dual or multiple use. Any competing claims should be rejected.

Your workstation should incorporate a telephone. If necessary an extension from the home telephone can be installed easily and cheaply. A useful addition to your equipment would be a telephone answering machine – especially a model which can relay messages to you when you are away and telephone in.

Rule 5 – Organise your support services

One of your basic but important decisions will be to determine the form in which you will present your written message. For a minority of jobs a typed letter might appear inappropriate – perhaps pretentious – and a handwritten submission will be expected. For the vast majority of appointments – certainly all those at supervisory, managerial, or specialist levels – an attractively designed and typed letter of application is mandatory. Printed letters are certainly over the top and convey an impression of an indiscriminate mailshot.

If you can type, even if with only two fingers, and you have a little cash to invest in your job search, it may be worth your while to commit some money to a personal computer with a word-processing facility. Choose a daisy-wheel printer, which will cost about £250. It pays to shop around. Some amazing discounts are available. Remember, though, that your computer should be a machine which stores information on hard or floppy disks, rather than on tape. By scanning such magazines as *Personal Computer World* (published monthly) you should be able to acquire a high quality personal computer, with word-processing software included, for about £200, making a total of around £450 plus VAT.

If you are not technically minded and fear that all this computer advice will be beyond you, or you cannot afford the word-processing equipment, do not despair. *Yellow Pages* will provide you with the names and addresses of several organisations able to offer you a comprehensive word-processing bureau service locally. Visit the various bureaus to explain your requirements – and to determine with whom you will feel most comfortable. If you are lucky you may know or hear of a professional secretary who can offer you a home-based comparable service from within your own immediate community.

Last, but certainly not the least, of your essential support services will be a good public library to which you have ready access. The commercial section should accommodate a wide stock of reference books, such as the *Kompass* volumes.

For specialist jobs, top positions, and/or appointments with small companies, you will need to consult a variety of other reference books. The *Personnel Manager's Yearbook* contains the names and addresses of the personnel executive in 500 major companies. The *Executive Grapevine* lists about 500 executive search and recruitment consultancies which collectively handle most of the senior appointments in the UK. Reference books, registers, and directories are published which cover companies and individuals within retailing, insurance, banking, brewing, accountancy, engineering, and a wide range of other activities.

The staff at your local library will be pleased to help you with suggestions and advice. If you are within easy reach of the City of London you will be able to use one of the best specialist libraries in the world – the City Business Library, which has just been relocated at 106 Fenchurch Street, EC1. (We discuss the interpretation of reference books and research information fully in chapter 10).

Rule 6 – Find yourself a counsellor

A confidential counsellor, with whom you can discuss your job search as it proceeds, can be of enormous help. You may feel your spouse or girlfriend or boyfriend may have sufficient acquaintance with the world of work to be able to fill that role, and may do it well.

If you have no one that close whom you can confide in, ask a suitable friend if you can talk things over from time to time. Another opinion could be very helpful in looking at the drafts of your marketing letters and c.v. It is also useful to have someone to rehearse you in the replies you are going to make to the questions you can be sure interviewers will ask you. You will have to tell the truth, but the way you present it can have an adverse or beneficial impact.

Ask your consellor to give you feedback on whether your replies are clear or confusing, whether you answer the question asked – or if you do not, whether the reply you give is relevant; whether you are long-winded or too abrupt, confident or hesitant.

You can also use your consellor to rehearse you in telephone technique – obtaining an interview by telephoning the company. Many advertisements have a telephone number at the foot of the advertisement. Companies which do not advertise their telephone number may still welcome a relevant telephone call that saves them the bother of sending out an application form, making judgments about it, and then making an appointment to see you.

Last of all, it is just sometimes useful to be able to talk over problems with someone else. The very fact of having to discuss the problem, to 'lay it on the table', can sometimes enable you to stand back and view it dispassionately, and hence make a better decision.

Job search counsellors

You will probably come across a number of firms that offer counselling services to people looking for employment, often referred to as 'outplacement counsellors'. They advertise from time to time in quality newspapers.

The better known outplacement consultants accept fees only from companies that are releasing staff, and who wish to sponsor redundant employees through a disciplined job search programme. If you are fortunate in working for a firm that offers you this help, accept it.

There are other outplacement firms that advertise for, and accept individual clients who are expected to pay fees themselves. Such outplacement counsellors are often expensive, and may charge up to 15% of your last salary as fees.

The facilities they offer may be good, but they cannot guarantee they will find you a job. If you are prepared to adopt a disciplined approach, and spend a little money on your own word-processing or photocopying facilities, telephone calls and postage, you can be as successful without incurring their fees.

If you consider using an outplacement consultant, obtain some telephone numbers of satisfied clients you can ring up, and check whether they thought the service was value for money before parting with your own.

Summary

Your six rules for organising yourself
1. Prepare a job search action plan.
2. Do not allow yourself to be diverted.
3. Provide yourself with office equipment.
4. Find yourself a workstation.
5. Organise your support services.
6. Find yourself a counsellor.

2

Keep Cheerful

An attitude is a way of looking at life – an approach which colours all that you think, do and say. Throughout your job search it will be of vital importance for you to remain cheerful in outlook and behaviour. Inevitably you will pass through phases of depression but your temporary despondency must not be allowed to show through and be interpreted as a lack of confidence.

The reason why you must generate an air of optimism is simple. Most people like a winner. Few like a loser. Think about all the popular people you know and consider how they differ from the unpopular people. Those who gather others around them, make friends easily, receive many invitations, and tend to be regarded as the life and soul of the party are invariably those who are cheerful, enthusiastic, display a sense of humour, smile frequently, and maintain regular eye to eye contact.

Such people are popular because attitudes are infectious. We all have the potential to be cheerful or to be sad, to be optimistic or to be pessimistic, but most of us like to be happy. Consequently we do not enjoy the company of morose, depressive, or humourless people who speak in a flat, lifeless voice and avoid your gaze. After all, who wants to be infected by negative attitudes, pessimism, or a pervading sense of gloom?

Obviously worries, illness, and protracted stress can adversely affect your demeanour and behaviour. For example, if you have just lost your job and are faced with a mortgage to pay and the expenses of children at school, the financial threat to your family security can be intimidating in the extreme.

Although full reassurance will not be forthcoming until you are safely installed in a well-paid job, you can alleviate most of the tension by taking *six basic steps*.

First, make an appointment with your bank manager and provide him or her with comprehensive information about all your finances and job search plans.

Secondly, if you have a mortgage explain your changed circumstances to the building society, bank, mortgage corporation, insurance company, or finance house which arranged your mortgage, and if necessary re-phase your monthly payments.

Thirdly, notify the Department of Social Security that you are unemployed and are available for work. Even if you do not obtain a job through your local Job Centre, you will be protecting your entitlement to Social Security benefits and confirming your status as an active job seeker.

Fourthly, confide in your relative and friends. Job offers can sometimes arise from local sources after a casual mention of the fact that you are in the market for employment. In any event, relatives and friends will be supportive and offer encouragement.

Fifthly, budget to spend the minimum possible during the job search process. Consign all your credit cards to cold storage until further notice by handing them to your bank manager for safe keeping.

Sixthly, check that the Department of Social Security are processing your P45, as you may be entitled to income tax rebates.

Once you have taken these steps you will feel more reassured in the knowledge that all sensible precautions have been adopted and you can embark on your job search with a greater sense of purpose. The blunt truth is that few, if any, interviewers will be interested in your problems. Most interviewers are busy people. Filling a vacancy will only be one of many tasks undertaken routinely by an interviewer. We all enjoy working with people we like. We do not care for those people who try to cast their burdens on us. Interviewers are no different from the rest of us in their feelings.

Any selector is likely to prefer people who are positive in their approach.

Once you have been offered a job interview, you will maximise your chances of success by approaching the challenge positively and adopting a cheerful attitude. Remember to be friendly yet not over familiar in your behaviour – and smile now and then.

An experienced interviewer will ask you questions which are designed to throw light on your attitude. These questions will be phrased in such terms as:- "What do you think about . . . ?" or "Tell me how you feel about . . . ?" When confronted with such questions, beware – quicksands lie ahead. You may be asked about your former employer, – perhaps the company from which you have just been dismissed unfairly or the organisation which declared you redundant unnecessarily. No matter how punitive your treatment might have been, never reveal what you may be thinking and feeling if those sentiments are negative and critical.

A catalogue of abuse allied to self pity may serve only to persuade the interviewer that you are a risky candidate with a 'chip on your shoulder' who should be avoided at all costs. No matter how heinous the crimes of your former employer, allow the interviewer to believe that as far as you are concerned you worked for a reasonable company, which may have hit adverse trading conditions, but which you were sorry to leave. Suggest that you derived considerable benefit from the experience which you acquired during an interesting and formative period in your working life.

As one personnel director explained: "I never recruit a moaner on principle, because I assume that such a person would be grumbling about us if we were reckless enough to offer an appointment. Furthermore I am not very keen about considering candidates who give me a 'hard luck' story on the basis that if bad luck runs in cycles I do not wish to introduce too much of it into our organisation."

Once you begin to think more positively and develop optimism as a habit, you will discover that your performance at interviews begins to improve significantly. Perhaps more importantly you may begin to feel differently about life in general. There is one way of looking at emotion (the James Lange theory) which suggests that we are happy because we laugh and we are sad because we cry. The emotion accompanies or quickly follows the bodily changes such as tears or laughter which are the direct result of the event or happening.

There is some truth in that theory. If you can say to yourself, "All right, so I don't feel cheerful but I am going to smile, laugh, and act in a cheerful way" you may quickly discover that your attitude grows more positive as the mask which you put on gradually becomes almost part of your personality.

Displaying a cheerful attitude is of real benefit in looking for a job. A colleague in our office introduced his daughter who had called in to see him. She was on her way to an interview for a post as a cook in a directors' dining room. "What interview advice can you give Judith in two minutes?" her father enquired rather flippantly. "Smile a lot", we urged, "and address the interviewer by name at least twice during the discussion. Interviewers generally like friendly people and enjoy hearing the sound of their own name".

When she returned from the interview she told us gleefully that the job was hers. "How do you know?" we asked. "You said that there were nearly one hundred applicants and you had been selected only for a preliminary interview from which the final shortlist would be drawn". "Yes", she explained, "but after about ten minutes the director who interviewed me said, 'You seem a jolly sort of girl. I am sure you would fit in here'. After another ten minutes he interrupted me to say 'Don't keep calling me Mr. Bridge, just call me Peter'. At that moment I knew that the job was mine!"

That true story conveys advice that may appear to be simple and basic – and so it is. Nevertheless some people seeking a job do need to hear the message and to learn from it.

Cultivating the correct attitude and maintaining a constructive outlook throughout your job search programme will not be easy. Almost inevitably you will suffer setbacks and periods of disappointment.

There will be times when you seem to be making little or no progress. You may have forwarded many letters to carefully targeted recipients and received a disappointing response. Remember that your activity rate and your sense of urgency will be more intense than anything which the people to whom you write might experience. The early offer of an attractive job will be an urgent priority for you. Executives, managers, and supervisors with jobs at their disposal could be faced with competing priorities, different from yours, and offering you an appointment may not be at the top of their list.

Some people are naturally more tense than others. A degree of nervousness can be advantageous – if controlled. Anxiety can be productive when it is generated from a desire to realise an objective and perform effectively. Outstanding sports people, entertainers, actors, and politicians have confirmed that their best achievements have frequently occurred when they were tense and apprehensive. 'Nerves get the adrenalin flowing' according to one Olympic coach. There are simple relaxation techniques which are effective. Controlled breathing before an interview is helpful for many people. Your local library should be able to provide you with a selection of guides on relaxation to suit your needs.

Avoid the temptation to seek reassurance in drugs and/or alcohol. If you are accustomed to a glass of wine or beer, continue the habit – provided, of course, that your budget is adequate. Any

15

increase in alcohol consumption should be regarded as a danger signal. In the final analysis, you will create and maintain the correct attitude to your job search task by a disciplined approach.

Summary

Six tips for creating and maintaining the correct attitude to your job search.
1. Try your utmost to be cheerful.
2. Even when you do not feel cheerful, endeavour to *appear* cheerful.
3. Train yourself to *sound* enthusiastic.
4. Smile during interviews and meetings.
5. Never relax by drinking alcohol before an interview.
6. Keep reminding yourself to think positively.

3

Know Yourself

As already mentioned (see Chapter 1), the process of self-analysis is an essential preliminary step in any successful job search programme. In order to know and understand the product (YOU!), this means subjecting yourself to a six stage process by:
- Reviewing your qualifications, skills, personality, and experience;
- Assessing your assets and strengths;
- Recognising your limitations and weaknesses;
- Defining the jobs which you are qualified to fill;
- Deciding what you would like to do ideally and
- Determining to whom you wish to offer and sell your abilities

Analysing yourself is a very difficult exercise. To obtain a relatively unbiased view of your personality, skills, experience and other attributes, you should ideally obtain a view from someone else – an objective outsider. Few people have the gift of seeing themselves as others see them.

Despite the inherent problems in attempting to look at yourself critically, you can make some progress by approaching the task systematically.

The reasons for undertaking self-analysis

The two main reasons why we are encouraging you to undertake a certain amount of self-analysis are that the discipline will:
- Prevent you from wasting time exploring areas of supposed employment that are unrealistic and
- Help to minimise the risk that, having obtained a job, you will later decide you do not like it for one reason or another.

17

Apart from the vocational self-guidance benefits, self-analysis can improve your interview performance. You will probably be asked by an interviewer to give some account of yourself and to describe what sort of person you are. If you have never thought about yourself critically before you may be at a loss for words and therefore create a poor impression.

How to start your self-analysis

To start your self-analysis, first of all make a list of your accomplishments. Detail your achievements – those things you have done well at work, college, school, around the home, on the sports field, or in your hobbies. These should be short specific statements using action verbs such as 'organised', 'planned', 'made', 'supervised', 'won', 'achieved', and 'controlled'. (We give additional information about this process in chapter four.)

If you have had employment, concentrate initially upon your work achievements. Take your time over this important activity. You will need this record later as a database from which to extract your career history or c.v. In chapters five and six we look at the uses of such statements in compiling a convincing c.v. Here we are considering them as a basis for analysing yourself; your strengths, weaknesses, aspirations, preferences, and dislikes.

When you have made a list of your achievements – those things which you have done well – you may find that you can group them in various categories. Think about them in relation to any preference you may feel for working with people on the one hand, and ideas and things on the other.

You may discover that you have been primarily a supporter of other people, a provider of technical knowledge, or a wise counsellor. You may have had positions as a leader, or as an organiser, or as an initiator of new policies and procedures. Alternatively you may decide that you are good at doing practical things.

After grouping your achievements into these various generalised categories, you will have identified some of your most important skills in the process.

For example, the following three achievements:
- Took over a small department of ten people, reorganised their duties and the work flow, and produced a 40% increase in output without increasing staff;

- Formed a local teenage football team, arranged fixtures, and refereed the matches;
- Started a neighbourhood watch system to combat local crime;

indicate that you are competent at *organising other people*,

Similarly the following three achievements:

- Helped the transport manager to choose the most appropriate fleet vehicles;
- Proposed a theme for the Christmas pantomime;
- Recommended two people to be local magistrates;

suggest that you might be successful and satisfied in an advisory rather than an executive role.

When you have identified your most important skills, begin to think about your preferences. Write a list of those things you may have particularly enjoyed doing, irrespective of whether you believe you performed them well or not, and see if you can generalise about them also.

At this stage some possibilities may emerge. For example, if you like organising others, are good at practical things, and have most enjoyed activities which took place in the open air, perhaps you should be thinking of jobs in the leisure industry, outdoor training, the armed forces, police, transport, civil engineering, fire service, or a range of roles which offer variety, involvement with people, and the opportunity to be out of an office or factory.

If what you have enjoyed is being part of a team, supporting others, and if you have no preference for outdoor activities, you may be best suited to a role which is office or factory based, involves group rather than individual tasks, and does not carry management or supervisory accountability.

What about your 'failures', if any?

Having examined your achievements, do the same for any failures you may have had, those things that you did not do so well. Ask yourself if they were due to personality clashes – and if so, which kinds of people do you clash with; whether they were due to any lack of ability on your part – always a difficult thing to own up to; whether you lacked experience or theoretical knowledge; whether you lacked interest and application in jobs you were given to do.

Such a study will give you some indications of situations to be avoided in future.

You should also consider whether your experiences in your last job leads you to consider changing your career direction entirely. If they do, then we deal with that subject later under the heading of vocational guidance. If, however, you reach the conclusion that your career path is broadly correct, then do not spend too much time in analysing your causes of past failures, if any. You can dwell too much on temporary setbacks with the danger that your confidence could be sapped as a result.

Once you have decided on the direction of your future career, concentrate at this stage on obtaining interviews. Once you have secured a new job there will be a short period in which it would be appropriate to analyse what, if anything, went wrong in your last job, and to make resolutions or form action plans to improve your prospects of success in your new role.

In any event, no two jobs are identical. Causes of failure in one may not necessarily be the same in another. A supposed failing in one role could even contribute to success in a different organisation.

Most people who need to find a new job try to resettle themselves by seeking something similar to their previous job. There is nothing wrong in this approach. For most people it is a sensible first step to pursue the familiar. This policy makes sense, however, only if it is realistic. For example, if your experience is within an industry that is contracting, and you are living in an area of high unemployment, you should consider other options.

Self-employment

Some job seekers will eventually decide in favour of self-employment. Depending on where you live and the intensity of local competition, there will be many or few opportunities for starting your own small business. There are several sources of finance available to enable you to launch a business. There are even some charitable grants to be awarded, especially to young people who have no capital at all.

Before deciding on such an entrepreneurial venture, however, you must be clear that self-employment will be more demanding than working for one employer, because each one of your customers will be your employer. It requires great self-discipline to work the long hours you need to make a success of the business and to control your finances. Until financial reserves have been accumulated it is wise to regard all but the basic necessities as 'luxury expenditure' to be avoided. Depending on the success of the business, money may flow in, but it has to be available to pay suppliers promptly when required, not to be spent on luxuries. Furthermore, if your business is to grow, you must be a good judge and manager of people in order to recruit and motivate competent staff.

Assessing yourself for the benefit of an interviewer

One of the questions often asked by interviewers is 'what are your strong points?', usually followed by 'what are your weak points?' At the very least, setting out your accomplishments should enable you to generalise about your strong points, and if challenged, substantiate your claims with convincing evidence.

In respect of those weak points which you have identified, it is helpful to memorise them constructively; but do not blurt them all out to an interviewer. Candidates are often taken at their face value, which includes the assessment they make of themselves. Of two otherwise equal candidates, one self-critical and truthful, and the other not, the less truthful might be preferred just because he or she does not sow doubts into the interviewer's mind.

Summary

Conduct a six-stage process of self analysis:
1. Review your qualifications, skills, personality, and experience;
2. Assess your assets and strengths;
3. Recognise your limitations and weaknesses;
4. Define the jobs which you are qualified to fill;
5. Decide what you would like to do ideally
   and
6. Determine to whom you wish to offer and sell your abilities.

4

Seek Guidance

We have already mentioned the role of outplacement counsellors, and suggested that, if you are not sponsored by your company, you may do as well by investing some of your money in buying a few guides such as this one and using the services of a word-processing agency.

However, if you are leaving school or college and are about to look for a job for the first time, or if you are dissatisfied with the direction your career is taking you and wish to change track entirely, you may consider seeking vocational guidance.

A session or two with a vocational guidance counsellor will result in your having a better appreciation of your abilities, aptitudes and potential, and how they might be best applied to the world of work. You may be counselled to try for jobs in a particular field, or with particular characteristics. You may be advised that you have the potential to obtain professional qualifications and where these might lead if you are able to undertake the study programmes entailed.

Good vocational guidance counsellors working in the private sector will often be chartered occupational psychologists. You can recognise them by their having the letters AFBPsS or FBPsS after their names. Consulting them is not cheap. Fees will probably be around £300. For that fee they will give you a searching interview, give you a number of psychological tests designed to stretch you in examining abilities and aptitudes, write a comprehensive report, and discuss it with you.

They will not be able to refer you to potential employers or colleges of further education. Those are contacts you will have to make for yourself, using methods outlined in this guide. However, they will dissuade you from attempting a career which you may find you later dislike, or in which you are unlikely to succeed.

It is always worth while seeing what the State will provide free. Counsellors in the State education or employment sector may have the advantage of being in closer touch with employers and the employment scheme generally.

Each Local Education Authority is required to provide a careers service in order to guide young school leavers towards suitable jobs in the local area. The careers service does have a wider function as well. There is no statutory age for people seeking advice. In each district there is likely to be a careers officer specialising in the problems and opportunities of 'older and abler' candidates.

Careers service counsellors are usually graduates who have undergone a rigorous training course at a university or polytechnic. They have available to them a range of psychological tests of which they have the exclusive use. These are tests of interests and aptitudes, and have been developed by psychologists in the Manpower Services Commission.

If you are an 'older or abler' individual you can request a consultation regardless of age. Naturally there are times when the careers service is under great pressure, especially in the two or three month periods prior to children leaving school at Easter and in July. But at other times they may be pleased to see you as a change from dealing with younger age groups.

The careers service offers one great advantage over private vocational guidance counsellors – their wealth of information on almost every conceivable career and industry. Careers officers regularly study jobs in the private and public sectors and prepare job descriptions and candidate specifications which are then circulated to all careers officers.

Every local careers office will have close contacts with all employers in that area, and will be able to refer you to a suitable firm. The careers officers can also find out about specific firms in your county or neighbouring counties.

If you are interested in a particular occupation, and want to know how and where you can obtain the relevant training, the careers service is one source of information you should consult. You will find the address of your local office in your telephone book.

Psychological tests and their uses

You are likely to come across psychological tests either as part of an exploration of your personal characteristics for career guidance purposes, or as means of obtaining more information about you by employer organisations. Some of the ways these tests can help you, or perhaps hinder you, in obtaining a job, and what to do about them, is outlined below. (We offer some practical tips on how to tackle tests in chapter 13.)

Most good professional executive counselling programmes will include some form of psychological testing and assessment. One rationale for this is that redundancy can be a time to take stock and decide what you really would like to do with the rest of your life, and to weigh up the possibilities of succeeding and being happy in doing it, bearing in mind your qualifications, experience, and temperament.

In making such decisions, self-knowledge of the sort that tests provide can be useful. There is no point in investing in a small post office type of business if you do not like dealing with detail to the extent that would be required, or if you are less than averagely interested in relating to people. Similarly, there is little likelihood you will succeed in a home-based computer programming job if what you enjoy is the stimulus of mixing with your peers.

Sometimes the problem is not so clear cut. For example, one of your options may be to become a self-employed life and pensions salesperson. If so, it would then be a good idea to have some insight as to your possible attitudes to being rejected by the people you call on, and whether a tendency to relieve stress with alcohol is likely to develop into a more serious problem.

However, most people faced with redundancy, and who have a problem relocating back into work, are usually those who are mature in years. Some of them, although perhaps not a majority, will know enough about themselves to be able to come to such conclusions without taking tests and having the results interpreted to them. For those who are able to contemplate a real change of life style, test results could be useful, either to reinforce their enthusiasm or to signal a warning light if the career choice seems inadvisable.

Most people who lose their job through redundancy do not seek some form of self-employment, even though that might be the best solution in their case. They seem to feel that they need to retain their standard of living and replace their previous salary with something equivalent. They believe it would not be possible to match a company salary, and the benefits that go with it, by earnings from self-employment. In addition, they would miss the day-to-day involvement with company life, and wish to continue to use the experience they have spent a career in acquiring. Perhaps the over-riding factor is that they lack the courage to strike out for themselves and to accept the apparent insecurity of self-employment.

They prefer to ignore their recent experience of redundancy, and to seek what they still perceive as the greater security of a job working for another employer. Only those who have been made redundant for the second or third time in short succession seem to have acquired a realistic degree of cynicism towards the corporate life, and are prepared to look at a real life-altering change of direction.

If you are an adventurous person, willing to explore the possibility of completely different life style, then a psychological assessment of your strengths, weaknesses, likes and dislikes, (based on tests, interviews and feedback and discussion) from a good vocational guidance counsellor, could prove invaluable. What if you are one of those people trying to pursue a career in the same line of business? Are tests of any use in such cases?

Tests can be helpful irrespective of your objectives and flexibility

If you are a person endeavouring to return to a corporate life, the experience of being subjected to psychological tests, and feedback and discussion of test results, can still be beneficial for two main reasons.

First, as more companies are using psychological assessment methods in their recruitment programmes you should have some idea of what you might be faced with. Whatever may be claimed about the fairness of tests, it is a fact that practice will improve your score up to a point. It may therefore be useful to look through books such as *Know your own IQ* and complete the examples. The same applies to personality tests. Many contain a form of lie scale so that inconsistent answers can be detected. If you have answered a few questions from personality tests beforehand you will not be put off balance by being presented with a personality questionnaire.

Secondly, there could also be more positive results. If people possess 'hidden' strengths which are revealed by tests, they may be able to steer themselves away from routine administrative occupations, for example, and to present themselves convincingly as strong candidates for high-energy innovative roles.

How then can you use test results to enhance your chances of getting a suitable job? After completing tests you are likely to be given an assessment report which will give you a framework for describing to an interviewer what your special characteristics may be. You can look through the report, be selective about its contents, and express a number of your characteristics as assets in certain job situations.

This process can be a useful confidence booster, and will also enable you to mention some of your characteristics in your c.v or application letter, when appropriate, in the knowledge that your statements can be confirmed by objective evidence.

Occasionally such tests can have a more 'directive' application. Recently we counselled an executive who had been a managing director of two companies in succession and was having to decide between two possible jobs: one as an MD again, and the other as a chairman of a group of small companies. Tests revealed that he was not a 'controlling, taking charge' kind of person, but rather he was a good supporter of others, willing to believe the best of people, and an encourager of others rather than an action-orientated person himself. We advised him, slightly against his own inclinations, to take the chairman role, where he has been both contented and successful.

Occasionally you may find yourself in disagreement with the test findings. Sometimes your perceptions may be more accurate. Nevertheless, the test will have been beneficial in provoking thought about the issue and in stimulating some self-analysis on your part.

Accordingly, if you are offered the opportunity to have career counselling which includes a psychological assessment in which tests play a part, you could find the experience valuable.

5

Plan your C.V.

There are three terms which are interchangeable – career history, résumé, and curriculum vitae, (or c.v for short). We shall use the abbreviation 'c.v.' as it is the term in most common use.

Why do you need a c.v.?

The c.v. will be your most important document, because it will constitute the basis for all your self-marketing activities. However, your c.v. will not win you an offer of a job by itself. There is no point in making your c.v. a complete definitive statement about the whole of your life to date.

Many people do not understand this. They tend to present a c.v. which may run to as many as six pages or more in the mistaken belief that the more they can write about themselves the better will be the document as a marketing aid. The reverse is usually the case. Long c.v.s may be interesting to the writer but can be boring to the reader. Its only function is to help you to obtain an interview. The interview is a crucial element in your job search because the decision to hire you will often be determined primarily by your performance during an interview.

Although most appointments are based exclusively on impressions drawn from an interview, this is not invariably the case. Astute and informed interviewers will use the interview to make judgments about your personality in order to determine whether you will 'fit in'. They will probe your ability to deal with hypothetical questions and situations, and analyse your previous work history and track record. Furthermore, competent interviewers will later check up on your main claims and assertions. Accordingly, your work history needs to be presented in an accurate but as favourable a light as possible, and in a form relevant to the needs of an interviewer.

As the way you present your career history can have a marked effect on whether you are called for interview it is obviously worth taking pains over its composition. Apart from basic personal and career information, your c.v. should indicate clearly what type of job you are seeking, and what kind of contribution you will be able to offer an employer.

The need for different versions of your c.v.

If you are applying for a standardised type of job within a number of similar companies, one version of your c.v. may be all that you require. If you intend to apply for a range of different jobs, or to approach companies which differ in size or type of business, then you will need several versions of your c.v.. Each one should tell the truth about you, whilst presenting the information slightly differently, or with changes of emphasis.

An obvious example of where more than one c.v. is essential occurs when students are applying for their first job. Sometimes they will reply to a question about the kind of job they are seeking with a statement such as:

"I am looking for a job in the financial sector, in stockbroking, in investment, insurance broking, merchant banking, or possibly commodity broking".

The career objective, as stated, comes across as vague and ill-considered. The recipient of a c.v. is more likely to be impressed by someone who seems single-minded about securing a job in a specific, defined sector. Using the same c.v. for each category of employer may just succeed in irritating all of them. The only way round this problem is to prepare a different c.v. for each market.

Select appropriate information

The selection of appropriate information and achievements to present to a particular company or range of companies in your c.v. must be predominantly a personal matter. Nevertheless you should show each draft c.v. to someone to obtain a preliminary and unbiased opinion. Your 'scrutineer' will nearly always have a constructive comment to make if you have chosen him or her well.

If you do not agree with his or her comments you are not bound to accept them although you should take note of them. It is easy for you to overlook some factor which someone else can quickly see should be corrected, omitted, put more succinctly or summarised in the final version.

At this juncture you will begin to recognise the advantages of having access to a word-processor, which can easily change areas and sections of the document for individual applications.

Prepare a 'database' of achievements

Before you can prepare a convincing c.v. you must assemble your database. First of all review your career, checking job titles and dates carefully to ensure that they are correct. Re-examine each appointment you have held and produce for each an 'achievement statement', listing all those things that you did well, or of which you were proud. You will need all this information when compiling your c.v.s and when preparing yourself for interviews later.

Wherever possible include hard, factual data like numbers of staff, or sales, or profits, or other statistics which will give a clear indication of the size of that achievement. Examples might be:

'Reduced the time taken in producing monthly accounts from seven to three days after the month end'.

'Designed and introduced a £150,000 computer network which saved six staff positions; reduced errors by a factor of ten; and achieved a payback period of three years'.

'Arranged a loan facility of £2m on a low fixed rate of interest of 8.5% at a time when interest rates exceeded 10% generally'.

'Handled 250 motor insurance claims a month'.

'Sold to 150 separate customers on average each day'.

'Dealt with over 200 telephoned complaints a week'.

No matter the field in which you may have worked, it should be possible for you to detail your achievements and also to indicate the significance of each major accomplishment.

When you have written your list of achievement statements (which is a task you may have to spread over a week or so as new items occur to you), you are ready to begin preparing your c.v.

The use of action words in achievement statements

When writing your achievement statements it is helpful to think in terms of your areas of activity. Consider such categories as planning, organising, controlling, and communicating. Within those groupings use action words such as 'developed, managed, planned, directed, supervised, achieved, designed, operated, controlled, administered, recruited, introduced, and completed.'

Using your database of achievement statements

The databank of achievement statements serves two main purposes. First, you will need it in order to select information for different companies according to what is likely to interest them. For example, you can extract significant and relevant achievements which would impress a new company. Secondly, the databank will also enable you to prepare systematically for an interview so that you can give specific examples of things you have done successfully in other companies. Without having previously searched your memory, and recorded and classified your successes, it is doubtful if you could remember, spontaneously, appropriate achievements in an interview.

Taking a look at achievements in this way may also give you an increased level of confidence. The realisation that a number of things you have undertaken, or tasks which you have completed, really have been significant achievements can improve your morale.

Your notes and listings should also include significant achievements in your life outside work. For example, it is worth recording any well developed interests which may have led you to organise events, canvass local support, administer funds, chair meetings or speak in public. Even if you have not done any of these things yourself, but have assisted and supported others who did, it is worth making a note of your successes in a supportive capacity.

Presentation

Recruiters are usually busy people. They do not enjoy spending time trying to read handwriting that may be difficult for them to decipher. Accordingly, in normal circumstances you should arrange to have your c.v. typed. Because you may need several different versions of your c.v., if possible have it typed on a word-processor where alterations can be made quickly and easily. If you cannot produce a typed c.v., then provided your handwriting is legible, write it carefully in black ink, biro or rollerball. This is because you may need to make several photocopies and blue and other coloured inks do not reproduce as clearly as black. Photocopies are acceptable provided they are made on good quality plain paper. Indeed, such copies can often look more impressive than the original document.

Always keep your master copies of each document in a clean folder and use a master each time you make further photocopies. Recruiters are often faced with photocopies of photocopies of photocopies. You must avoid poor presentation because an interviewer may equate poor presentation with a poor candidate.

You should always use white A4 paper and, in order to produce the highest quality presentation, you should photocopy on to 100 gm paper. Although you will probably find that you can buy 100 gm A4 high quality paper only in boxes of 500 sheets (a ream), the expense will represent a good investment. You will also need a supply of white envelopes, of a reasonable quality and of a sufficient size so that your A4 sheet of paper does not have to be folded more than twice. Envelopes are generally discarded by the recipients once the mail has been opened so you can use envelopes of lower quality if necessary.

Summary

Five guidelines to remember when preparing to write your career history:–
1. Decide how many different versions of your c.v. you will need.
2. Collect appropriate information.
3. Prepare a 'database' of achievements.
4. Write achievement statements.
5. Ensure that your presentation is of the highest quality possible.

6

Write your C.V.

When you have completed all the preparatory steps (as explained in chapter four) you will be ready to write your c.v. In order for your c.v. to prove successful – and obtain interviews for you – it must satisfy two tests. First, the content must be appropriate and comprehensive. Secondly, the c.v. must be written in an attractive and effective style.

Personal details

The start of your c.v. should contain essential personal details, such as your name, your address, and (sometimes overlooked) contact telephone numbers, both at home and at work. A prospective employer may wish to fill a vacancy quickly and consequently attempt to make interview arrangements by telephone.

If you are outside the optimum age range for a job and are aged, say 53, it may be advisable to include your date of birth in a section headed 'Other information' at the end. Unfortunately age discrimination is widespread in the United Kingdom, but by adopting this tactic the selector may have noticed something of particular interest in the opening paragraphs and have already decided to see you, before he or she is tempted to discard your application solely on age grounds. When it is eventually noted you are 53, your age may still be a 'turn off', but it is possible that you may be invited for interview anyway. Although indicating your age at the end will not guarantee you slip through the net, it may increase your chances, even if only slightly.

If you are clearly outside the age range specified in an advertisement, should you conceal your age altogether?

There is probably little point in being evasive. The company placing an advertisement may receive over 50 replies anyway. If the employer regards an age over 45 as a firm disqualification, such an employer will deduce from the other information given roughly how old you are. In any event, if you are aged 53 you probably should not be relying on advertisements to win you interviews.

Could you conceal your age by omitting dates altogether from your c.v.? The idea, whilst ingenious, is unlikely to help. Selectors have little patience with what they consider to be vague or evasive applications and may suspect that you have concealed more than your age – a spell in prison perhaps!

If you really have been in prison, then it may be inadvisable to produce a c.v. at all. There are some consultants who believe that a c.v. can be disadvantageous anyway, as it reduces you to the same mould as everyone else. An imaginative letter, with some achievement statements, may comprise a better approach than the conventional c.v. – especially if there are personal 'difficulties' which you need to cloak and if necessary explain at interview.

Include a short 'Career summary'

Following the opening section on personal details, which could include marital status, ages of children, and your date of birth (if 'acceptable') you should then set out a 'Career summary' statement. The career summary statement, which should be a short, concise paragraph, provides an invaluable opportunity for you to make a favourable judgment of yourself. This evaluation should provide the reader with a brief interesting overview of your career and thereby encourage him or her to read the rest of your c.v.

Examples:
"Having been top of the form in mathematics throughout school and with a strong practical interest, I decided to become a cost accountant."

"Having qualified at an early age, I was offered . . . "

"With a sound sales and marketing management background gained in the . . . confectionery company in the UK, I was headhunted for a general management role in a market-driven organisation . . . "

"Following an apprenticeship with one of the most skilled engineering firms in the area . . . I was promoted to section leader at 22."

Follow the career summary with an 'Aims' or 'Career objectives' statement

Your career summary, together with an 'Aims' paragraph which can be separate or combined, will help the reader to decide where you might fit into the new organisation. You may wish to change your career direction slightly, bringing together various strands of your experience to bear in a different direction. The reader may need your help to see you in this new light. Unless you clearly state your aims and indicate the value you can bring to a new company in a new role, you may just be considered for 'more of the same', because it will be assumed that you are seeking a role similar to your most recent job.

Examples:

"With a broad engineering apprenticeship, five years in sales and marketing, and a knowledge of finance gained from private reading and two intensive management courses, I am seeking an appointment to run a small division or profit centre within a larger group where I can use the full range of my skills."

"Having concentrated on management accounting, I am now seeking a broader role as a financial controller embracing both financial and management accounting."

The career summary and aims statements can be varied and adapted to appeal to a range of companies to which you will be forwarding your c.v. It is difficult, if not impossible, to fit an aims and objectives statement to the needs of more than, say, 20 similar companies. As you tackle different sections of your potential job market you will need to present your skills and experience in different forms.

The same advice will apply to other sections in your c.v. After all, if you were invited to complete a standard application form issued by several different companies, no doubt you would be selective about the way you presented career information to each of them. Similarly, when making direct applications using your own c.v.s, you need to match your career messages to your audience.

'Work history'

Once you have completed your personal details, written your career summary and aims statements, and prepared your list of achievements, you can begin to assemble the rest of the information. Your next section should be 'Work history', which will comprise a chronological list of employers, starting with the most recent and working backwards.

Each reference to an employer should state the name of the firm and its location and also indicate the size and nature of its business. It is dangerous to assume that the reader will deduce this information from the name of the company. If he or she does not know anything about your company, but is conversant with the activities of another candidate's employer, he or she may conclude that the experience of that other candidate is relevant. In those circumstances the reader of your c.v. may not bother to research into your own previous experience. Consequently you run the risk of losing by default. The secret is to provide sufficient information without becoming verbose.

With a line, or at most two, set down the company's name and the dates you worked there. If you are going to be pushed for space, try putting these dates at the right of the page on the same level as the name of the firm rather than in the left margin. You can then lay out the information without having to indent it under the name of the firm, which will create a better visual impact. (See below).

You should include your job title, and if you progressed from one role to another, highlight the most recent job title and in the text briefly explain your progression. For example:-

Franklin & Howard, Watford   **1983-1987**
Sheet metal fabricators   Turnover £5 million   130 employees
Plant foreman, promoted from chargehand. Responsible for all
production of alternators and generators from drawing office
specifications, sales £1.5m.
Streamlined the production line, improving . . .

You will find this format takes up less space than the alternative attractive layout, thus

1983-1987   Franklin & Howard, Watford
            Sheet metal fabricators   Turnover £5 million
            130 employees
            Plant foreman, promoted from chargehand. Responsible
            for all production of alternators and generators from
            drawing office specifications, sales £1.5m.
            Streamlined the production line, improving . . .

If space is not a consideration you may prefer to use the more spacious presentation style, which most recipients will find attractive. You must plan the layout of your c.v. to ensure that it does not extend to an additional page on which a few isolated lines appear. A c.v. which is untidy could alienate the reader even though the track record of the applicant otherwise might be impressive.

If you wish to include a lot of information to strengthen your application, careful layout planning could prevent your c.v. from running into an unnecessary extra page. With each job reference you should include two or three achievement statements which you perceive are *relevant* to the needs of the company to which you are applying. Such achievement statements need not necessarily relate to what you regard as your most significant successes. Beware of the temptation to emphasise the achievements in which you personally take pride. Remember you are endeavouring to arouse the interest of a prospective employer in your ability to satisfy the needs of that employer. Relevance must be the over-riding test!

What other information should you include or omit?

The next section of the c.v. will be determined by your own background. For example, you may include a section headed 'Education and qualifications'. On the other hand, if you cannot point to any examination passes and/or qualifications, you might be well advised to omit the section. After all, you do not want to draw attention to your deficiencies and weaknesses.

If you have some strong interests (especially where you can point to awards, prizes, or other successes) you may decide to include a separate section labelled 'Interests'. Where your interests are less significant you may mention them in a general section – 'Other information'.

Interests

Is it useful to mention interests at all? Will some employers hesitate to recruit someone whose life seems dominated by outside activities, thereby leaving less energy and enthusiasm for the job? As a generalisation, it is likely to be beneficial to your appliction to mention interests.

An indication of hobbies, sports, and other leisure activities will give the interviewer something to discuss as a warm-up topic, and something to ask about if he or she runs out of work history questions – or if, as with students, you have not yet had the opportunities to create a track record.

There is some truth in the expression that 'if you want something done, give it to a busy person'. The extent to which you have pursued your interests is regarded by some interviewers as a clue to the strength of your motivation, drive, or general enthusiasm for life. It is widely believed that a person who is strongly motivated in one area is likely to be energetic and enthusiastic in other areas.

If your interviewer has been trained in interviewing techniques he or she will have been encouraged to look for evidence of both involvement and achievement in interests, together with successes in work history. Consequently he or she may ask a number of probing questions. So do not claim as interests or hobbies activities which hold an appeal for you, but of which you have no deep knowledge. You may be regarded as an exaggerator, even something of a fraud, and then other valid aspects of your work history will become suspect also.

Do not include bizarre or emotionally sensitive interests unless you are quite sure about the identity, interests, and attitudes of the person by whom you are going to be interviewed. The chairman of one large London firm of insurance brokers happened to be keen on embroidery. He would take his latest embroidery to work on during long plane journeys. Whether a junior male broker applying for a job in that company and stating that one of his interests was embroidery would have been recruited is doubtful – unless it were the chairman who interviewed him. If the applicant were a girl most interviewers would regard embroidery as an appropriate interest. A young male candidate with embroidery as a hobby might have been rejected by anyone other than the chairman.

All your recorded interests should appear appropriate, or at least not counterproductive. If you are applying for a job in the City and you are a member of the Labour Party or CND, a discreet silence about your convictions could be advisable. On the other hand, if you are looking for paid employment with a charity like Shelter, or the Child Poverty Action Group, membership of the Young Conservatives may amount to automatic rejection. Prejudices exist in all organisations and can colour or distort decisions.

Education

If you obtained three or more CSE, GCSE or GCE 'O' level passes at school in academic subjects, they may be worth mentioning, depending on the level of the job. If you obtained two or less, it may be better not to mention them and let the interviewer assume, if he or she does not probe, that you achieved acceptable results. In that case, just state the name of your school and dates you attended. (On the other hand, two such passes could be regarded as a recommendation for some routine or lower-level jobs, and therefore would be worthy for inclusion.)

If you are under 35, and have no other qualifications, 'A' level passes should always be detailed, unless you are applying for a very senior job when you may decide to omit them. If you possess a degree it will be assumed that you have 'A' level passes at university entrance grades. Consequently, it is hardly worth recording them unless they could be relevant to the job or the company's business. In that event specify them all. For example, the company you are approaching may have an export business. If your degree was in English, it would be beneficial to indicate any 'A' level passes in Spanish, French, German or other living language, even though you may have ceased studying the subject formally at 18.

Providing details of your school and university can sometimes be tricky. Anyone will be acceptable if they have been to Oxford or Cambridge, even though Oxbridge used to suffer from upper-class connotations. Restricted information may be advisable if you attended Eton or Harrow, for example. Some interviewers will relate to you instantly if they discover you are an Old Etonian or Old Harrovian; others might decide that such a background is a disqualification! You may inflict less self-damage if you refer to 'a public school education from age 13 to 18'.

Other information

Under 'Other information' can be included those items which you think that you should report but do not feel you need to highlight, in case they might be regarded as prejudicial to your application. Such 'risk factors' might include age, religion, a divorce, or membership of a club or a stag hunt. Even possession of a Private Pilot's Licence irritates one quite well-known selection agency interviewer (who presumably does not possess one himself). The secret is to avoid controversial and/or suspect issues which an interviewer, who may have all kinds of prejudices, could find offensive.

A different approach

So far we have been discussing a c.v. which takes the reader through the applicant's career in a logical date order. This kind of c.v. does not always display the applicant in the most favourable light. For example, a number of rapid job changes may raise doubts in the interviewer's mind about the candidate's 'staying power' and stability. Will the candidate remain only a short time with the company if appointed, with the result that the recruitment exercise will have to be repeated all over again?

A track record as a 'job-jumper' does not necessarily reduce your chances of employment in junior posts. One example we can quote is that of a woman, now aged 40, who regularly has had 10 different jobs a year. She is intelligent, has taken further qualifications at evening classes since leaving school, and has always been highly regarded wherever she has worked. As a creative, multitalented person she finds that the boredom factor rapidly sets in. Consequently she resigns to seek a new challenge. She has worked for nearly all the High Street retail multiples, for a bank, two building societies, has sold cars for a local garage, and had several jobs as a telephonist/receptionist. Some of her employers have been so impressed with her capabilities that they have contacted her after she left (for the first time) and persuaded her to rejoin them. Despite special appeals she remained only for a further short period after each re-engagement.

With a career record like that, a chronological c.v. would cover several pages, and would almost certainly disqualify her for any further employment, or even consideration for a vacancy.

The only way to overcome this problem is to prepare a 'functional c.v.' which groups your accomplishments under different headings and classifications. For example, our multitalented woman could choose at least four broad categories – administrative tasks, clerical work, sales experience, and receptionist/telephonist duties. She could be highly selective about the number of accomplishment statements she provided so that it does not become apparent how many different employers she has worked for.

With a track record that many interviewers would regard as appalling, her problem in finding alternative employment is to put herself in front of an employer who has a need for some of her skills, and make an impression by virtue of her adaptability and attractive personality. If you have a track record similar to hers you may do better, like her, not to have a c.v. at all.

There are literally thousands of employers who adopt an unsystematic approach to recruitment, and their lax screening process may be easy to slip through. Even local branches of big companies will take short cuts when their need for staff is desperate. Obtaining an interview by registering with an agency, or calling on a company that is advertising, particularly a small company, may be all that is needed to secure a job offer.

At senior levels the functional c.v. can also be effective where entirely opposite circumstances apply, such as the senior executive who appears to have limited experience because he or she has only worked for one company, and therefore may seem 'institutionalised'.

If you have a record of long service with one company, a list of chronological appointments in that company may not make a favourable case for consideration. A functional c.v., grouping experience under different functional headings, can be a more convincing way of describing your relevant and varied experience.

Do not include salary details

Whatever type of c.v. you may decide to use, do not include your salary history, or other salary information. Details of former salaries very quickly look out of date. Unless the interviewer applies a discounted cost of living factor, it may seem that you have been poorly paid, perhaps because you have been a poor performer, or held an inferior position.

You should not include details about salary requirements either, because they can harm your prospects in two ways. You may rule yourself out from further consideration if the company thinks your salary requirements are going to be too high. On the other hand you may be excluded because it may be assumed that somebody whose salary expectations are low is not likely to be of sufficient skill level to succeed in the role under consideration. There will be plenty of time to deal with salary questions in the interview or in subsequent discussions. Just keep reminding yourself that the c.v. is essentially a tool designed to obtain you that interview.

Supplying references and meeting honesty checks

Most employers will take up references on you, and particularly in respect of senior level appointments that you may have held. Thorough employers and/or recruitment consultants will also check any degrees or professional qualifications which you claim. Making a false claim could disqualify you, even though you may be able to succeed in the job on your own abilities. We have to include this warning because in our experience as recruiters at least one in 20 candidates claim false qualifications, and about a quarter cleverly exaggerate the level of their qualifications. Pass grades are converted into credits or distinctions for example, and unclassified degrees 'acquire' a good classification.

Similar tendencies apply to salary and bonuses earned in previous appointments. Your past aggregate remuneration can be independently deduced from your P45 which you have to present to a new employer on joining. If you have exaggerated your income, and the discrepancy is discovered, you may be lucky and the company may decide to take no action.

Many companies include a clause on their application form requiring you to certify that the information which you have given is true. Even if an employer does not discover immediately that the information that you supplied was untrue, nevertheless your dishonesty could still provide legal grounds for terminating your contract without any compensation.

References are frequently required from both personal referees and from employers (invariably your current or last employer, but sometimes previous employers also). Select your personal referees carefully. As consultants we have occasionally approached personal referees, with the prior permission of a prospective candidate, only to discover that the reference was damning. Invariably the message was transmitted verbally rather than in writing. Two typical examples were:-

"Yes, Neville did ask me to act as a referee, and I did not like to refuse. He is certainly very bright, but unfortunately he quickly becomes bored with any job. If you want someone to beaver away at a job indefinitely he is really not your man."

"Joan mentioned the job to me and said that she needed a referee. I am very friendly with her husband and had no option but to agree. Unfortunately she has had a drink problem which she has struggled to overcome. I believe that she has now succeeded, although it has left its mark."

Do not assume that a personal referee will communicate to an employer in the way that you would wish. Check with your personal referee about the message to be transmitted. If you have any doubts about his or her co-operation attempt to clarify your reservations with the intended referee. As a last resort you may need to approach someone else with whom you can be sure that you can establish mutual trust and joint understanding.

Almost certainly you will have less control over the selection of employer referees. Despite the inevitable constraints you should endeavour to influence whatever might be said about you so that you are presented in the most favourable light. Ideally you should know what *will* be said or be written about you. We strongly advise you to draft a reference for discussion with your present boss, and previous bosses where possible. If any intended referee does not agree with the wording of the reference you have drafted, try to discover exactly what is likely to be said. It does not matter too much if it is uncomplimentary provided that you are forewarned about the contents of the reference, whether written or oral.

When you submit a draft to your boss or an ex-boss, keep it short and to the point. Ensure that it emphasises what you believe were your strengths, and refers to any of your significant achievements. The reference would be especially helpful to you if it were to say, for example:- "We would strongly recommend him/her for any post requiring . . . (and then followed by a list of your favourable personal qualities).

If you know that the comments to be made about you are likely to be adverse, they can be defused by warning your interviewer in advance and giving your version of the facts. For example, you may be able to say in response to a question about references:-

"My boss will probably say that I was headstrong and rebellious and failed to consider others' feelings. There could be some truth in that but please remember that the company's need to get things moving was paramount. If I had followed his civil service background of doing nothing without carefully preparing the ground in case it rebounded, there would have been a commercial disaster".

You must prepare the interviewer for any damaging comments about you. If he or she has been warned that they will be made, and then they do occur, then the harm will be minimised and the impact softened. The referee will only be confirming what the interviewer has already been told, and the interviewer may have been expecting more critical comments! Many executives do not welcome surprises. They are busy people and prefer 'predictabilities'.

An executive who receives an unfavourable reference, when he or she has been led to believe that a favourable reference will be forthcoming, is likely to react adversely. Do not prejudice your chances of an appointment by creating false expectations.

Writing your 'marketing letter' to accompany your personal history

The most important item in your job seeking campaign is your c.v. The second most important is the letter you will send with it. However, although an effective c.v. may take you a long time to prepare, an individual letter can be drafted quite quickly.

The ideal marketing letter will say three things:-
1. That you are looking for a new position.
2. Why you are writing to that particular company or institution.
3. What you can do for them if they appoint you.

Some of what you say may be duplicating parts of your c.v.,but do not be concerned about that. C.v.s and covering leters can become detached from each other. A copy of your c.v. could be circulated to other executives without any accompanying explanation and must be capable of standing alone as a marketing document in its own right.

Some outplacement counsellors who have not changed their methods with the times will advise you to write to senior executives in companies on spec – in itself a good tactic – but asking for an appointment in order that you can be given some advice about your career.

Asking for advice is one tactic we advocate when 'networking' and is useful in that context, discussed later. Indeed, several years ago that strategy may have succeeded in gaining you an appointment with complete strangers which you might then have turned into a job candidacy. But in the last 15 years so many similar letters have been generated by the clients of outplacement consultancies, all of whom tend to follow each other, that the approach has become worn out.

It is acceptable to ask advice from people you know, or to whom you have been introduced directly or indirectly. This is different from asking advice from strangers. Once you have been talking to someone and told them a little of your history, it seems quite reasonable to ask them where, in their opinion, you should be making approaches. They may have up-to-date knowledge of which companies are growing or contracting in their field, or what skills are currently in demand. But that presupposes you already have an introduction. It is presumptuous to expect busy executives to deflect attention from running their companies and to spend time talking to some unknown person who ostensibly has no desire to become a candidate for a job with their organisation.

In any case, subterfuge to obtain a job interview under the guise of asking for advice is both undesirable and unnecessary. As we explain in the next chapter you can obtain interviews by more systematic and orthodox methods.

Examples of ineffective and effective c.v.s

Being well qualified does not necessarily ensure that you will be a sought-after candidate. Much depends on the way in which you present the information about your career.

As an example, the two c.v.s that follow were produced by a young man who had left Oxford with a first-class honours degree but who had postponed job hunting until after he had finished his final examinations. He wanted a career in the financial sector and had been thinking about banking. He had applied to all the clearing banks, most of the merchant banks, several overseas banks, and a few insurance brokers, all without success.

On discussing what he wanted from a career it became apparent that his needs would be better suited by a job in insurance broking, and we advised him to concentrate on that. We counselled him on more effective ways of finding a job, as outlined in this book, including how to set out a c.v. His first attempt at a c.v. aroused no interest at all. His revised version obtained him a job he wanted in less than four weeks.

His first version of a c.v.was boring, and did not help a selector to relate the candidate's background to the world of work. Also, if he was attempting to find a job in insurance broking, an occupation where successful people are generally light on education, mention of a first-class honours degree would be thought of as a negative indicator.

The following quotation from his 'thank you' letter to us shows the importance of writing an interesting c.v., adapting it to fit the industry, toning down achievements if necessary, and of making unsolicited direct applications:

" . . . As you will have gathered from this, (my news), by following your advice closely, I had little difficulty in finding a job after months of trying other methods, and would like to express my deep appreciation . . . "

If you do not have a sound academic background, as he did, consider how much more important it may be to impress the selector with what you can do!

Only his name, and the dates and the names of his school and college have been altered to disguise his identity.

Original ineffective version

CURRICULUM VITAE

Roger William Chorley   Born 2nd January 1966 in London
Nationality: British   Single
Address: 35 Onslow Street, London W4R 3GJ
Education: 1979 – 1983 Radley College, Abingdon
    'O' levels: Latin (A), French (AI), Italian (A)
    1984 – 1988 Queens College, Oxford
    1st Class B.A. Hons in Modern Languages (French and Italian)

Awards and Prizes: Doncaster Scholarship in Modern Languages (Entrance); Academical Clerkship; Heath Harrison Travelling Scholarship; Mrs C. Beddington Prize; Paget Toynbee Prize; four college prizes.

Work Experience: Jan – June 1984: Translator/Trainee with *La Fondiaria Assicurazioni* in Florence.
Oct 1986 – May 1987: English Language Assistant at Lycée Janson de Sailly, Paris.
Much freelance translation work from French and Italian into English, including 2 weeks at the BBC in April 1987.

Interests and Activities:
    School: Monitor; President, Archaeological Society; active member of CCF (Instructor); member of school choir; 2nd XV rugby.
    University: President O.U. Italian Society; active member of French Club; Member of Queens College Chapel Choir; college rugby; member of various university choirs; squash; flute and guitar; organisation of the visit of a French theatre group to Oxford.

Revised effective version

CURRICULUM VITAE

Roger William Chorley   Born 2nd January 1966 in London
Nationality: British   Single
Address: 35 Onslow Street, London W4R 3GJ
Career Aspirations:
Having recently completed an education which has enabled me to meet a variety of people, to travel, and to develop a wide range of interests from music and drama to politics and rugby, I am now seeking to embark on a career in finance. I am anxious to acquire a good training and if possible study for an appropriate professional qualification so as to form the ground-work for a career in which I could make good use of my academic skills and have the opportunity of meeting people and negotiating with them. Rather than seeking immediate high financial rewards, I am anxious to lay the basis for an eventually successful and rewarding career.

Work Experience:
October 1986 – June 1987
As an optional part of my course I spent this period working as an English Language assistant at Lycée Janson de Sailly, Paris.

I was responsible for supplementing the teaching of English to pupils preparing to enter the 'Grandes Ecoles' and business schools. Quite apart from the experience of working closely with others, I was able to meet a wide cross-section of French society, get to know the country, and perfect my language.

January – June 1984
Before going up to university I worked as a translator with *Fondiaria Assicurazioni* in Florence.

Here I gained experience of producing accurate and detailed work under pressure, and of being responsible for the accuracy and quality of my work. I also gained some insight into negotiation through interpreting for foreign visitors to the company.

I have also worked extensively as a freelance translator, learning in the process how to work under my own motivation, and to strict deadlines.

Education:
1979 – 1983 Radley College
1984 – 1988 Queens College, Oxford BA (Hons) in Modern Languages

Interests and activities:
President of the Oxford Italian Society, organising meetings, lectures, films etc. I was much involved with a variety of musical activities and also played rugby and squash regularly.

My principal leisure interests are musical and they have taken me on tours of Holland, Germany, and Austria as a member of a choir and soloist. My interest in theatre helped me to join a theatre group in Paris in 1987 as a musical accompanist, and I organised a visit of the same group to Oxford in 1988. I am at present preparing for them to perform in Oxford and London in February 1989.

Summary

Points to remember when constructing your c.v.
1. Decide whether you need a chronological or a functional c.v.
2. Design several versions of your c.v. for different job markets.
3. Include in your c.v. :-
   - Personal details
   - Short career summary
   - Aims or career objective statement
   - Work history, supported by achievement statements
   - Interests
   - Education
   - Further education and qualifications
   - Other *relevant* information
4. *Do not* include salary information in your c.v.
5. Avoid false and 'exaggerated' claims.

7

Secure Interviews

An essential interim step towards obtaining another job is to secure an interview – preferably a number of interviews. With few exceptions (*au pair* appointments, for example) vacancies are filled only after a face-to-face interviewing process has been completed. Accordingly, all your initial activities must be directed towards obtaining interviews with potential employers or their intermediaries. Your career history or c.v. should be designed to produce interviews at which you can sell yourself and convince the interviewer of the benefits which will follow from employing you.

So how do you set about winning those interview appointments? There are five main methods.

1. Replying to advertised vacancies

Vacancies are sometimes advertised on radio, on television, at the cinema, on noticeboards, at shops, in programmes, leaflets and booklets, through professional journals, and by various other unusual methods. The vast majority of all advertised vacancies are notified through local, regional and national newspapers. Some of the advertisements will appear over a box number with the identity of the prospective employer disguised. If you are unemployed you cannot afford to disregard the anonymous advertisers. An organisation may have a valid reason for cloaking its identity. On the other hand, if you are in a job you may need to be wary – just in case the advertiser is your own employer!

Do not assume that you will know automatically the publications in which relevant advertisements will appear. Personnel executives are becoming more imaginative and less predictable when selecting their media. For example, senior appointments are increasingly advertised in the regional, rather than the national, press. This trend could intensify as geographical disparities in house prices widen, removal costs rise, and relocation problems become more intractable.

That ideal job which you seek might just be advertised in an unexpected publication. As it is impracticable for you to buy every possible newspaper and magazine, regular visits to the reading room at your local main library are essential. With practice you will quickly acquire a 'skimming technique' which enables you to scan the columns without overlooking those advertisements which could be relevant in your job search. Most libraries will allow you to photocopy extracts from papers and magazines at nominal costs. (If your library does not offer this service, request its introduction).

When you have assembled your advertisements, do read them carefully. All vacancy advertisements will contain an 'action point' telling you how to respond. An application procedure will be outlined. If you are requested to telephone for an appointment do not forward a lengthy letter. Do not write to the managing director if you are asked to obtain an application form from the personnel manager. You may regard the procedure required by the advertiser as bureaucratic or inappropriate but you are not making the rules. You cannot afford to ignore or bend them. (You will find details about advertising techniques and how to respond to them in chapter eight.)

Some advertisements will contain details of specific skills, qualifications, abilities, or experience which are described as essential or desirable. If you respond to an advertisement of this type, it is beneficial to refer to each such item in your covering letter and explain briefly how you meet the defined criteria.

As we have explained (in chapters one and ten) you must organise and classify all your documentation and papers. Cuttings or photocopies of advertisements to which you respond, copies of your letters, the application forms which you complete, and any supporting information must be dated, classified and filed. Delays may occur before you receive replies from companies. Sometimes your letters will be ignored unless you operate a follow-up system which will ensure that you send a reminder. When you do succeed in securing interviews, your cuttings and photocopies will be vital material in preparing yourself for successful interview performances by comprehensive personal pre-briefing.

2. Exploring the hidden job market

Replying to advertisements is relatively straightforward. A company has a considered need, defines that requirement in print, and you respond. Unfortunately, from your point of view, many other people will respond also. A well-written advertisement appearing in the national press will probably attract something around 50 replies, although the range can extend widely from 15 to 50 to 500. Consequently you may be in competition immediately with about 49 or more other people. It would be surprising if there are not 10 or so of those applicants who are as well qualified as you.

If you pass the initial screening process and a first interview, there are still likely to be two or three other candidates on the subsequent shortlist. There are ways of reducing the competition, but many job seekers have not thought through the options and confine their job search to answering advertisements.

In answer to survey questions about how well their job-seeking activity was progressing, people have expressed satisfaction with their efforts by saying, for example:-

"Although I have not yet received a firm offer, things are going quite well. I have replied to 30 advertisements, had eight interviews and been short-listed four times".

We would not be satisfied with such a record, not even if we had been short-listed 30 times. Indeed, that degree of 'success' would be a cause of great concern, because it would indicate that something was severely wrong with our interview technique. There are no prizes for coming second on a short list. There is only one winner – the person who is offered the job.

All that can be claimed after a series of unsuccessful interviews in competition with others is that such a person probably has acquired some comprehensive interview experience.

Put yourself in that person's shoes and then consider this proposition. How much easier you might have found the process if there had been only one candidate – you – especially if you had been able to submit yourself as a candidate before the person specification was completed? You might have been able to prevent the inclusion of so-called 'essential' requirements (such as age limits) which are not relevant to successful job performance, yet effectively will prejudice your chances of selection subsequently.

Fortunately the hidden job market contains numerous vacancies which will provide you with opportunities to exercise your initiative and be one or more jumps ahead of your competitors who confine themselves to the inertia of the press vacancy market. Exploring the hidden job market is a task which demands persistence, imagination, and careful planning. The activity is so important to you that we have devoted the next chapter to the subject.

3. Obtaining an interview by telephone

Each year a large number of interviews are obtained because job-seekers take the initiative and telephone selected companies directly. A surprisingly large proportion of such interviews can, and do, lead to the formal offer of a job.

One retail operations controller explained to us that he frequently arranged to meet people who telephoned him about employment. "I like people to ring me directly because that demonstrates that they have had the motivation to find out that I am in charge of this division, and then have had the confidence to ask for me by name. Usually I inform a caller that I can spare ten minutes for a chat. If after the ten minutes I think the person has something to offer I will either extend the discussion into a telephone interview, or, if I have a busy schedule, arrange another appointment. I have recruited eight or nine people by this method. It is cheap and quick – and so far all these appointments have proved successful. So why should I spend money on advertisements and expensive consultants when I have no need to do so?"

No doubt the people who approached the retail operations controller conducted some personal research into the company and its key executives before making the call. Knowing the identity of the director, manager, or supervisor whom you should telephone is crucial. You must ask for the key executive by name, and if necessary, by job title also. The identification of the appropriate executive may be difficult, but persistence allied to imagination will usually unearth the information you require.

The telephone switchboard in each of your target companies will be able to help you in most cases. Ask the telephonist or supervisor for the name and job title of the person in charge of the department, division or section to which your employment objectives relate. If the name and/or job title is unusual, check the spelling carefully with the telephonist or supervisor. Occasionally you will find that the switchboard staff cannot, or will not, provide the information – either because they do not know the organisation structure in detail, or because they are too busy to be deflected from dealing with routine calls. In that eventuality ask to speak to the public relations manager or to the company information office, who should be familiar with every part of the business and know the key executives personally.

Do *not* ask to speak to anyone in the personnel department, otherwise you will run the risk of the standard response – "Oh! You are looking for a job. Forward your c.v. and we will consider it in the light of current vacancies." Once you have allowed yourself to be manoeuvred into that position you have lost the initiative and have been reduced to another career summary in the personnel department databank.

When you have ascertained the name and job title of the key executive, you can either ask to be transferred to his or her extension, or you can thank the supplier of the information and ring off. Sometimes you may wish to collect your thoughts, or conduct further research before making your approach to the key executive. When you do make your approach your initial message must be brief and to the point. Every second over one minute will diminish the impact of your initial message. Consequently you should pre- pare the message carefully and rehearse it several times.

One message which quickly produced three interviews and one job offer ran as follows:- "Mr Adams, my name is Lorraine Lawton. I am ringing because I have managed DIY stores success- fully for four years. Your new merchandise range interests me and I believe that I could improve sales and store profitability. I am looking for a new challenge and would like to join your team. I can send you a c.v. but I thought it would save time if I could have a brief discussion with you." This type of message was invariably well received, even in those instances where no interview resulted.

You may be confronted by one difficult obstacle when tele- phoning the key executive – his or her secretary! Some secretaries are extremely protective and believe that their prime duty is to screen their boss from the world outside his or her office. Such secretaries will put through calls only when there is no alternative. Normally the secretaries will attempt to deal with enquiries them- selves or deflect them to another department. When you telephone you will be asked to indicate who you are and what is the purpose of your call. Comments along the lines of the following may help you to overcome the secretarial hurdle.

"My name is Brian Peters. I am an expert on production engineering. I would like two minutes of Mr Collier's time to exchange views on a matter which I think would interest him."

If the secretary presses you further you could try:- "I am sorry, but as the matter is complicated I really need to discuss it with him personally." The secretary may still be uncooperative. Your next step might be: "It is not about insurance." That should be your last ploy. Extricate yourself diplomatically and live to fight another day by adopting the following approach:- "I realise from your questions that Mr Collier is a very busy man. When would be a better time to phone him? Will this afternoon at about 3 p.m. be convenient?"

With determination you will be able to reach about 60% to 70% of your target executives, managers, or supervisors. Self-marketing by telephoning is one invaluable technique for the job seeker. The method has been tried and tested successfully in other fields also. Indeed, life assurance sales persons and financial advisors acquire a substantial proportion of their business and earn high fees, by adopting a similar approach. Of course, you must be prepared for the inevitable rebuffs – and the occasional hostile or rude response. Console yourself with the reflection that the working environment in such companies is likely to be unpleasant anyway!

4.   Networking – one of your key approaches

With the growth of outplacement consultancies, 'networking' has become a common term. Although the term is generally assumed to be American in origin, the concept is identical in principle to the long established and frequently derided 'Old Boy Network', which has prevailed in the United Kingdom for at least two centuries. Networking describes a process whereby one contact leads to another and the extension of the net eventually results in a good catch (that is, a job!) The 'Old Boy Network' still functions strongly and many top appointments are made this way.

Networking could prove to be the most productive single technique in your job search programme. There are seven steps in the process:-
1.   Write down the names of every business person known to you who works for a company or public corporation in a position of authority.
2.   Write down the names of everyone known to you socially who holds a position of authority.
3.   Telephone all the business people known to you to seek advice about where you should direct your self-marketing activity.
4.   Obtain brief appointments *at the office* with your selected

business people where possible. The executive will have his or her list of contacts at the office and, if necessary, will be able to pass you over to another manager who might be more knowledgeable about your field. Furthermore, you have a better chance of converting your enquiry into a job candidacy in an office atmosphere than during a telephone conversation.

5. Telephone all the people you know socially, who hold any position of authority, and arrange to meet them informally – perhaps at home or over a drink.

6. Explain to both your business contacts and your friends that you are seeking a change of employment. Briefly outline your skills, experience, qualifications and any of your strong 'selling points'. Probably you will be able to speak to your friends more confidentially. You may even be able to convert one or more of your friends into a counsellor.

7. Seek *advice* from all your business contacts and your friends. You need not feel embarrassed in making such requests. Most people like giving advice. They do not like being asked for favours – but they will not regard the provision of advice as a favour.

In following the seven-steps networking process there are several tips to follow.

First, do not assume that your skills, experience, abilities and qualifications will be known to your friends and business acquaintances. Because you are familiar or close terms with someone it does not follow that he or she is aware of all your strengths as a job applicant. They see you in different contexts. You may be modest by nature. Nevertheless, some self-promotion and personal advertising is essential – although perhaps in a diplomatic manner by 'casual points' and 'informal reminders'.

Secondly, seize every opportunity to advance and progress enquiries a stage further. Here are some examples. You have arranged a brief exploratory meeting with a business contact. There are no appropriate vacancies in that company, although your contact has suggested several companies which you could approach. Follow up with an enquiry along these lines:- "Thank you for those helpful suggestions which I will certainly pursue. Do you know the names of the key people I should approach?" If names are forthcoming, move to the next stage. "Would you mind if I mention your name?" By this stage you will have obtained, indirectly but effectively, introductions to companies. You will then be able to telephone the nominated executives in those companies and say:- "x in company y suggested that I might telephone you. He (she) thought that you might be interested in my . . . . "

Or your business contact might say:- "I have enjoyed our chat and have been impressed by your background as a laboratory technician. Unfortunately I don't think that we have any vacancies just now." Here is an opportunity for you to suggest:- "I am grateful for the trouble you have taken and do not want to waste any more of your time. Would you mind if I organised a short chat with your research and development manager? Even if there are no vacancies, I would be pleased to talk briefly about some of the projects we handled in company Z". Then, if and when you meet the research and development manager, you will arrive with the semi-endorsement of the business executive.

The networking technique is adopted by successful sales people. They tend to describe the process as 'referred leads'. Those leads can be obtained in several directions. Within a company, you might find that the referred leads are upwards, downwards, or horizontal. Again you could be offered referred leads to other companies, associations, individuals, or a combination of several potential sources.

Thirdly, regard executive search consultancies and recruitment consultants as part of your networking system. Executive search consultancies and recruitment consultancies use the networking system in reverse. They are searching for people, rather than searching for jobs. They regularly telephone selected companies and their many other 'sources of information' to collect names of potential candidates for vacancies known – and unknown.

Executive search consultants ('head-hunters') operate at the highest levels of the recruitment market. Unless you are, or have been earning at least £25,000 per annum in 1988 terms, you would probably be wasting your time and energy by approaching head-hunters.

Recruitment consultancies tend to serve managerial levels, or below, and should be used if you are seeking a job between, say, £12,000 – £30,000.

Specialist employment agencies confine their activities to distinct sectors. An employment agency recruiting pharmaceutical staff and another recruiting nurses are typical examples.

Irrespective of the type of recruitment consultancy, or the operational level, all have one characteristic in common: they find a large proportion, if not all, of their candidates by a variety of techniques other than advertising. With the astonishing proliferation of executive search consultancies, recruitment consultancies, and employment agencies, of every description, you may experience some difficulty in finding your way through this jungle. (We offer you some advice in chapter ten, 'Research the market'.) *When you have determined your appropriate 'consultancy strata' and selected the consultancies, approach them all.* We have often been asked by job-seekers: "Which are the best consultancies?" The question is irrelevant! A surprisingly large number of recruitment consultants and 'head-hunters' have had little or no training in interviewing and selection techniques or the measurement of human abilities. Nevertheless, the less competent consultants may be the most successful in winning assignments because they are highly efficient at marketing their services. From your standpoint *any* consultant with attractive and suitable jobs in his or her portfolio is a good consultant!

Fourthly, ask executive search consultancies and recruitment consultancies for advice in your job search. Consultants are often busy people, although their workloads can fluctuate substantially. During slack periods they may be prepared to give you their time in advising you about ways in which you might improve your interview performance and marketing plans. Often they will be able and willing to point you in the direction of prospective employers known to them but unknown to you. Obviously they will 'keep you for themselves' if you happen to match one or more vacancies which they are currently handling. Candidates are the lifeblood of any successful executive search or recruitment consultancy. Expert marketing may secure contracts but repeat business will be forthcoming only if the assignments are completed successfully by the appointment of suitable candidates.

5. Making casual calls

This is not a method which we would recommend as a 'mainline activity'. It is rather like making your investments in Premium Bonds. 'Ernie' does pay out some winners regularly, but the odds against your success are substantial.

It is possible to succeed in finding a job by a casual visit occasionally – provided that you can offer a scarce and readily measurable skill. For example, the following applicants were all offered, and accepted, an appointment after unannounced visits to companies known to us – a computer programmer, a systems analyst, a graphic designer, a commercial artist, a sales representative, an interior designer, and an animator.

All the candidates were drawn from occupations in short supply, and where individual ability could be objectively assessed promptly. For example, three of the candidates carried a portfolio of their work with them: their creative ability was open to immediate inspection.

Unless you possess a rare skill which is highly marketable and readily measurable you should concentrate your efforts on seeking a job by more productive methods. By all means make the occasional casual call if you have some spare time in between appointments, or if you suddenly feel motivated by gambler's hunch. After all, long shots sometimes pay off. As Peter Drucker has said, "Miracles occasionally do occur, although they are not a highly reliable management tool". The task of finding the correct job for you is a management exercise. To succeed, you will need to concentrate on priorities and manage your time efficiently.

Summary

Five methods to consider when seeking to obtain interviews:-
1. Scrutinise advertisements in all media and apply for appropriate vacancies.
2. Explore the hidden job market.
3. Telephone selected executives in selected companies.
4. Use 'networking' extensively.
5. Make casual visits where possible.

8

Study Advertisements

Finding the right people

From the employer's point of view there are many ways of finding applicants and filling vacancies. They include:-

Internal staff transfers	Job centres
Staff promotions	Staff recommendations
Professional registers	Casual enquiries
Employment agencies	Company files
'Head-hunters'	Advertising

Thus advertising is only one recruitment method – although it is not one which you can afford to ignore. The person preparing a vacancy advertisement normally will have one main objective – *to attract a manageable number of suitable candidates*. Busy executives can see no virtue in enticing large numbers of applicants (especially if most are inappropriate), thereby merely generating an unnecessary and unwelcome workload. In designing and drafting their advertisements they will endeavour to deflect unsuitable candidates without causing offence or damage in terms of public relations and company image.

Where to find the advertisement for the kind of job you are seeking

Advertisements are not as easy to track down as they were ten or fifteen years ago. Personnel managers are displaying greater imagination in their choice of media today. The media possibilities embrace:-

Local radio	Brochures

National radio	Posters
Regional T.V.	Exhibition displays
National T.V.	Cinemas
Prestel	Press advertisements
Leaflets	Sandwich boards

The most popular form of media for recruitment remains the press, although the pattern is changing and evolving information technology might alter preferences further.

Britain enjoys a reputation as one, if not the greatest, of the world's press nations. Whilst the proliferation of publications might be beneficial in terms of public information, the task for you, the job seeker endeavouring to locate appropriate advertisements, can be arduous. The advertisements which you need to read might appear in a variety of publications, for example:-

National dailies	Trade and technical magazines
National Sundays	Academic publications
Regional dailies	Careers publications
Regional Sundays	Directories
National weeklies	Newsletters
Local weeklies	Guides
'Freebies'	Special supplements
Professional journals	

In the past personnel managers were inclined to advertise in the 'high-profile' expensive press because they believed that the prestige of a national advertisement would generate a good response. Indeed, it has been said that the *Daily Telegraph* and *The Times* were able to prosper during circulation wars largely because of the extravagant and uncritical expenditure on vacancy advertisements by personnel executives! Today it is widely recognised that excellent recruitment results can often be achieved by utilising specialist journals, local and regional newspapers, trade and professional magazines, and 'off-beat' publications.

You will need to screen as many publications as possible. The first rule is not to attempt to buy them all. Unless you are wealthy you will not be able to afford the newsagent's bills – and even the prosperous job seekers will not welcome the creation of a personal waste-disposal problem. Rely on your local library, develop your own 'skimming technique' to scan publications quickly, and enlist your friends to keep their eyes open for any likely advertisement.

Beware of the temptation to accept unnecessary constraints – the

"Thursday is the *Financial Times* day for accountancy appointments" concept, for example. Whilst you should look at the *Financial Times* on a Thursday if you are seeking an accountancy role, you must read the *Financial Times* on every day. A financial director known to us said:- "I know that Thursday is *the* day for finance jobs in the *Financial Times*, that is why I *never* advertise on a Thursday. Companies do not beat the competition by following the herd. They succeed by being different – not by being the same. I do not want my advertisements to be overshadowed or lost in a mass of advertisements running to two or three pages. I either advertise on a Saturday, when readers are relaxed anyway, or use a local newspaper. On one occasion I assembled an excellent shortlist from two sentences in the personal column of a weekly magazine."

Dissecting the advertisement

Once you have located an advertisement which seems appropriate to your job search, you will need to dissect the advertisement in order to understand the intentions of the employer, and also to detect the hidden messages. Many vacancy advertisements require translation. Their clichés, jargon, stock phrases, and exaggerations have become source material for Britain's alternative comedians. 'An exciting opportunity for ambitious self-starters in a thrustful marketing-led, dynamic company'may really mean 'This is a dead-end job in a company which has been badly managed and is now moving from confusion to desperation.'

The 'hype tendency' has intensified for two main reasons. Today most personnel executives do not write, or even draft, their advertising copy. They rely on the services of advertising agencies within which copywriters prepare 'marketing messages' which are intended to 'sell' jobs to prospective candidates. Most of the agency copywriters have had no direct experience of job analysis, interviewing, and selection. Frequently their background has been restricted predominantly to service with an advertising agency where the emphasis would have been on selling products or services to a consumer market by presentation techniques. The point at which exaggeration degenerates into misrepresentation or dishonesty is difficult to detect. Nevertheless, an increasing proportion of job advertisements in the national press appear to be in danger of contravening the objectives of the Trade Descriptions Act and the Code of Advertising Practice guidelines.

The second reason for the 'hype expansion' is that the disease is infectious. At a recent staff selection seminar two thirds of the delegates (all drawn from personnel management positions) confessed that they regularly overstated the significance of, and challenge within, any vacancy which they advertised. Typical comments were:-

"Yes, I accept that I overstate all the attractions and disguise all the liabilities. On the other hand, everyone is up to the same game. If I tell the truth, the whole truth, and nothing but the truth, I won't finish up with a short list." or

"You cannot introduce strict objectivity and honesty unilaterally. If we manage to entice some people into the company by using a few 'white lies' what is wrong with that? We can always attempt to condition them once they are aboard and we have got to know them better."

If you are in urgent need of a job because you have been unemployed for a lengthy period or your current role has become unbearable, you may be willing to ignore the hype. Nevertheless, it may be helpful to estimate the extent of the exaggeration factor. Research into previous advertisements and/or discussions with current or former employees can be revealing. For example, if a role continues to offer 'outstanding promotion prospects' why have three people resigned from the position and the company in the last five years?

Experienced and informed personnel executives will include six factors in their vacancy advertisements. It is useful to understand the strategy of the advertiser when planning your own job search campaign. The six elements of an advertisement are as follows:-

1.   Factual information about the role
Details about the job title, reporting relationships, key tasks and remuneration are usually accurate (although salary prospects are sometimes 'enhanced').

2.   An outline of career prospects
This is a common hype area. Any careful scrutiny of the national press advertisement pages will indicate that the vast number and array of 'unique career opportunities' and 'unrivalled promotion prospects' on offer cannot match the actual growth and development of many of the companies. A careful reading of company annual reports (which you can obtain free of charge on request to

the head office of each company) can often provide you with more objective information to counteract press optimism and advertisers' licence.

3. A definition of essential requirements in the ideal candidate
Normally any 'essential requirements' are so defined because the company could not contemplate the appointment of anyone who does not possess the 'essential requirements' under any circum stances. 'Must be able to drive a car and possess a clean driving licence' or 'verbal and written fluency in French' are stipulations which do not leave you, as an applicant, with much room for manoeuvre.

4. A description of desirable requirements in the ideal candidate
These are attributes which the interviewer would prefer you, as a candidate, to possess. They are not mandatory, however, and someone who is a little below standard on one or more of these desirable requirements could be offered the appointment if suitable in other respects. Consequently you have scope to 'angle' your c.v. and covering letter so that you reassure the prospective employer. You should be able to compensate for any possible deficiences in your track record by emphasising all your strengths and achievements.

5. 'Preselectors' in the advertisement
Experienced personnel managers will include in an advertisement restrictions and limitations – commonly referred to in the profession as 'preselectors'. Their aim is to 'screen out' unsuitable candidates before they become part of an unnecessary, embarrassing, and excessive workload. Clearly if the 'preselectors' are expressed in the form of essential requirements (as explained earlier) you will be wasting your time if you do not possess the specified skills, knowledge or experience. When fluency in French is stipulated as essential and you can only struggle with 'holiday French' you will not be able to become bilingual before the interview date! On the other hand, there may be isolated occasions when you can persuade an advertiser that given a brief learning period, you would have the ability and motivation to acquire the requisite attribute.

6. 'Encouragers' in the advertisement
Advertisers realise that the people who read vacancy advertise-

ments tend to fall into three broad categories: self-motivated people pursuing job opportunities; casual readers 'skimming the columns'; and personnel executives, recruitment consultants, and remuneration specialists attempting to keep abreast of current trends. Companies recognise that some of the best potential candidates (from their point of view) may not be actively seeking a new job. 'Encouragement items' are inserted in the advertisement in order to convert lukewarm 'skimmers' into firm applicants by arousing their enthusiasm. Sometimes advertisers are tempted to overelaborate or exaggerate facts in order to claim the attention of casual readers. You should be aware of this tendency and use your judgement in applying a corrective 'discount factor' when analysing the advertisement and assessing your own suitability as a prospective applicant.

The design of vacancy advertisements

Vacancy advertisements are designed and presented in many different forms. One common construction is illustrated below:

ATTENTION SEEKER
(Headline)
REFINING FEATURE
(Sub-Heading)
Company Description
Job Description
Person Requirements
Incentives
Action Point
Address

The factors are not necesarily described and displayed in sequential order.

Sometimes the job description and the person requirements are portrayed 'side-by-side' as follows:

The Role	*The Person*
The key tasks include:-	Ideally the candidate will:-
● _____	● _____
● _____	● _____
● _____	● _____
● _____	● _____
● _____	● _____

Your reactions to the advertisement

The quality and content of your response to the adverisement will probably determine whether you are offered an interview or not. Remember that at this stage your aim is to secure an interview. Your behaviour at the interview is another issue (which we discuss in chapter 12). There are three important rules when replying to the advertisement.

*1. Reassure the advertiser about your capacity to meet all the specified **essential** requirements.*

Provided that the general response to the advertisements is adequate in terms of numbers the short-listing could be determined mainly, or solely, on the basis of one test ' 'Does he or she possess the specified essential requirements?' If the answer is 'No' that could be the end of your candidacy. Some ingenuity might be necessary on your part when submitting your application – *but you must reassure the company that you can satisfy the 'essential' demands* by one method or another.

2. Convince the advertiser that you can meet most of the specified desirable requirements either immediately or in the near future.

The advertiser may use 'specified desirable requirements' as a short-listing test if there have been numerous applicants and a substantial proportion have already cleared the 'specified essential requirements' hurdle. Accordingly you should consider the desirable requirements carefully and *attempt to write something about each desirable requirement, provided that your statements are true and you will be able to substantiate them at a subsequent interview.*

A competent interviewer will explore all, or most, of your written declaration. False or exaggerated claims on one point (which could be of minor importance to you) might destroy your credibility generally and/or raise doubts in the mind of the interviewer which cannot be resolved.

3. Study the 'action point' thoroughly and follow the instructions.

The vacancy advertisement will contain an 'action point' which can take one of several forms, for example:–

'Write to . . . '
'Telephone . . . '
'Write or telephone . . . '
'Forward your c.v. to . . . '
'Write a short letter explaining why . . . '

'Submit a brief career history . . . '
'Telephone for an application form . . . '
'Write for an application form . . . '
'Meet our representatives at . . . '

There are many other possibilities. *No matter how unusual, or inappropriate, the procedure appears to you – adopt it faithfully.* If you are interested in the vacancy you must follow the recruitment rules which the company has formulated. When you have been offered and accepted an appointment with a company you may be able to comment upon, and influence, the future recruitment methods of your employer. So long as you are a candidate, compliance with the regulations is to be strongly recommended!

Hidden messages and 'added value' from vacancy advertisements

You can often draw useful conclusions from vacancy advertisements by searching for the 'hidden messages' and 'added value' statements. With imagination you can often unearth job opportunities – and be one jump ahead of your potential competitors. For example, a declared requirement for several salespeople could indicate an impending need for additional sales office staff. Recent advertisements by a major construction company for two project managers and four project engineers led to 64 subsequent appointments as the support teams were assembled. Accordingly, all vacancy advertisements which are expansion-oriented in their presentation and content are worthy of serious scrutiny, whether or not they seem appropriate to the kind of job you are seeking.

Companies which are growing will often tend to fill the top jobs first. They do so not only because understandably they are concerned about the most important roles, but also because they may wish to allow executives to be involved in the recruitment of their own support teams. When new executives arrive on the scene, they will welcome 'waiting' applications on file from prospective candidates who will be capable of helping them. You may face some delay between making your speculative application submissions and the arrival of new executives. Nevertheless, the employment prospects for you can be significant, even if slightly delayed.

Similarly, expanding companies can be frequently identified by the sheer volume of vacancy advertisements. Of course, you will need to deduce whether the multiplicity of advertisements is a reflection of low morale or an indication of steady expansion. Speculative applications to growth companies are often successful – and may result in appointments which offer significant promotion prospects.

Summary

Seven tips when studying advertisements
1. Screen widely.
2. Include 'unusual' sources.
3. Dissect the advertisement.
4. Look for the 'essential' requirements.
5. Look for the 'desirable' requirements.
6. Note the action points.
7. Extract the hidden messages.

9

Look for Hidden Jobs

Vacancies can arise in many different ways. Frequently the cause is outside the control of the employer and the event may be completely unexpected. For example, a person suddenly resigns in order to accept a job elsewhere. Or an employee suffers a serious accident. Illness which is unusually protracted can necessitate the replacement of a member of staff. A company may be awarded a large contract which requires the urgent recruitment of additional staff. An organisation may be invited to provide a new service or to develop an improved product – major tasks which will involve the prompt introduction of new skills and experience into the company.

Such vacancies are arising all over Great Britain every working day of the year. Obviously the roles will very widely in content and seniority. They will tend to have one factor in common – they will be regarded as 'extremely urgent' by those directors, senior executives, managers, and supervisors who are suddenly confronted by an unexpected recruitment need. Obviously the organisation will be under pressure to take some prompt action. The 'remedy' could be the hurried preparation of a 'job description' and a 'person specification'. The task could fall to an overloaded executive, a busy personnel manager, or an external recruitment consultant. A person specification will emerge by one route or another which will define desirable and essential skills, qualifications, experience, attributes, personality traits, and physical factors. The job specification and the person specification will be considered, approved, and confirmed. At the point of ratification, the documentation will tend to become 'frozen in authorisation'. Amendments and variations will then be difficult to achieve. Whether the vacancy is to be filled by a press advertisement, through a 'head-hunt' or by some other method, the criteria for selection will have been predetermined and be beyond your influence. For example, you may be 55 but an upper age limit of 45 has been stipulated. Over 60% of all advertisements for senior executives specify an age range of 30-45.

As the personnel director of a medium size mechanical and engineering company explained:"In common with many other personnel executives I always impose a declared age limit of 45 in order to confine the number of applicants to manageable propositions. If I were to permit 55, say, as the top bracket, I would be inundated with applications and thereby merely make myself an unnecessary and excessive workload. That is not to say, of course, that I would always refuse to recruit someone in their fifties. As a matter of fact, I recently offered quite an important job to a man of 57 who was recommended to me by an outplacement counsellor. There is no way, however, in which I would ever contemplate extending age ranges in advertisements to embrace people of 57".

No matter how great the pressures on an organisation, there is usually some gap, or 'window', between the period at which a recruitment need is first perceived and the time at which the job description and the person specification are prepared. The more senior the role, the wider the gap, or 'window', is likely to be.

A managing director known to us was dissatisfied with his company's marketing and sales results. He reviewed several possible courses of action. He considered transferring his advertising and public relations manager to a different job. He thought about changing the advertising agency. Organisational solutions received his careful examination – the possible acquisition of a smaller but growing competitor; the regionalisation of the sales force; the removal of the marketing director; and a combination of two or more of these possible courses of action. All this deliberation occupied nearly two months of analysis and investigation. Throughout this period of enquiry he retained an open mind, whilst reflecting on the best way forward. Eventually he decided to ask the personnel department to strengthen the marketing department by the recruitment of an assistant head of department.

At that point the characteristics of the 'ideal candidate' began to be defined on paper in precise and narrow terms. Imagine what the managing director's reaction might have been if he had received an approach, during his investigation phase, from someone who seemed to have relevant knowledge and experience? At least the managing director would have been interested – and probably interested enough to arrange a meeting with the person. During the subsequent discussion the managing director might have quickly converted his visitor into a candidate in his own mind. At that stage, it could have appeared sensible to the managing director to explore ways in which he could utilise his, now, 'candidate' to alleviate the difficulties confronting the company. From that point, it is but a short step to the joint formulation and structuring of a job description and a person specification which will identify what the company needs ideally from a candidate, and to modify those demands in the light of the abilities which the 'candidate' can reasonably be expected to offer.

The moral to be drawn from these illustrations is that a direct approach to an executive with a job to offer can be beneficial for you in at least three different ways:-

- First, the direct approach can secure serious consideration for you as a job-seeker, whereas your responses to job advertisements might only produce routine and (sometimes delayed) bureaucratic rejections.

- Secondly, your direct approach could enable you to influence the key executive, or executives, before a job description and a personal specification have been prepared. Thereby, rather than expect a candidate to adjust to the job, you could help to shape a role to fit the person: you!

- Thirdly, your direct approach may have the effect of eliminating potential competition. As a chairman of a major leisure group explained when subsequently appointing a sales executive who had telephoned him directly – "Only one person can fill a role, therefore why delay if a suitable person is sitting opposite you?".

In a company with which we have been associated, half of the top management team which controlled subsidiary companies had attained their positions by some form of direct contact, introduction, or recommendation. You, too, could 'create your own job'. What is the secret of success? First, in order to obtain interviews in the 'hidden job market' you need to believe that out there in the world of work there are employers with needs which you are competent to satisfy. If you are not entirely convinced of that, you must still be prepared to give the idea a serious attempt. Secondly, you must be willing to invest about £150 in the exploration of the 'hidden job market'. £150 is the approximate cost of two or three career histories presented in different form, photocopies, paper, envelopes, and 250 postage stamps. When you have organised yourself for this important task you must 'identify' as many companies as possible which might have an employment requirement which you can meet.

How do you find these companies? The answer is not quite like finding a needle in a haystack, although luck does play a significant part. There is no known method by which you can identify the ideal target companies for certain. If it were possible to 'spot them for certain' you could reduce your workload substantially and perhaps content yourself with approaches to a dozen companies. All you can do in practice is to recognise potential employers. Your objective is to narrow that unlimited number to a sensible target list. Several 'refining systems' can be used to limit the field – selecting companies by geographical location, size, industry, function or some other classification.

Some occupations are highly 'mobile' in application. For example, drivers, accounts clerks, personnel managers, financial controllers, security staff, company secretaries, sales directors, marketing managers, receptionists, auditors, computer programmers, systems analysts, engineers, and many other staff find that their skills, experience, and qualifications are ready transferable across different industries. Such people are not restricted to working within a narrowly defined sector. Conversely others possess specialist abilities which, by their nature, do not permit universal application. Within reason a computer specialist can 'go anywhere'. A creative flavourist will be restricted to employment in the food industry unless he or she is prepared to make a complete career switch.

You will have to determine your appropriate 'catchment area', based upon your own conclusions about geographical location, company size, the type of business, and the products or services. There is no substitute for your own personal research, aided by the support which you can derive from your local library, your counsellors, and your informed friends.

A useful starting point for your research will be the Extel cards which you can find in the commercial section of any good library. The essential, basic information for about 5,000 companies is summarised on the cards. You could scan them quickly, in alphabetical order, and note the names of those companies which seem to merit further consideration.

If you are not mobile in terms of work location, and wish to be employed in a specific area, you should pay special attention to the comprehensive *Kompass* directories. Companies are categorised by several classifications, one of which is geographical location. Consequently you could use *Kompass* to indicate all the organisations in your chosen locality and then supplement that information by referring to the Extel cards from which you can extract your target companies.

The *Kompass* publications are invaluable for personal research, but they do not cover all sectors of the U.K. economy. If you believe that your talents and experience will be of direct interest to a particular industry, you should scrutinise the relevant trade directory. For example, if you can offer retailing expertise you need the *Retail Directory*, published annually. Again, your library will help you with the provision of appropriate directories and other works of reference.

Once you have chosen your first 20 target companies you will be in a position to select that version of your two or three forms of c.v. which will be best suited to each target company (more about that later!) You will also be able to choose one of your various draft covering letters to accompany your c.v.

The next step is to contact the most senior line executive in each target company who is likely to have the authority to make a decision to employ you. For example, if you are seeking a job as a personnel officer, for large companies on your target list you should write to the personnel director. In small companies you should approach the company secretary or general manager. If in doubt about a choice from two or more executives, always write to the most senior executive. For top management positions, and many specialist roles, it is advisable to contact the chief executive rather than the personnel director.

A personnel executive may be under pressure to meet tight deadlines – an industrial relations problem, perhaps, or a salary review. Almost inevitably a letter from you will be relegated to the back of the queue. The chief executive usually faces pressures of a different type. Although he or she will be accountable for vital decisions, by definition they are likely to be fewer in number than those taken by subordinate managers. 'More important decisions, but few of them', in the words of a pharmaceutical company's managing director. That particular chief executive always found time to read letters from job applicants. Furthermore, in common with other managing directors, he possessed the authority to make appointments and to review and change organisation structures.

A letter to such a person can land on the chief executive's desk when a 'hidden vacancy' is 'turning over in the mind of the chief executive' – unbeknown to the personnel director. The same letter addressed to the personnel director might be considered at a later date, and then only in relation to vacancies known to the personnel director. Obviously a busy personnel executive may not feel disposed to bother his chief executive with an application for a vacancy which has not yet crystalised into a job description!

Of course, most enlightened professional personnel executives will already be aware of departments in the organisation which need strengthening. Indeed, such perceptive personnel executives are likely to exercise an initiative by suggesting the creation of new roles. In any event, from the job-seeker's standpoint, a letter addressed to a chief exccutive is more likely to be passed downwards to the personnel executive than a letter addressed to the personnel executive is likely to be passed up to the chief executive. Your application to the chief executive has a better chance of remaining a 'live document' than a similar letter forwarded to the personnel director who, after all, is more accustomed to filing applications in the databank!

The choice of recipient for your letter of application must be a matter of judgement for you. The form of address leaves no scope for initiative. You must address the person to whom you decide to write by his or her name, ensuring that the initials are correct, the job title accurate, and the company address correct. If in doubt on any detail, telephone the company to check the information before you forward your application.

Summary

Five preliminary stages in your potential job identification programme.
1. Conduct comprehensive research to determine your catchment areas and target companies.
2. Select the appropriate version of c.v. for each target company.
3. Select the appropriate version of your covering letter to accompany each c.v.
4. Identify the target recipient of your c.v. and covering letter in each company by name and by job title.
5. Keep detailed records of every application which you forward and every reply that you receive.

10

Research the Market

As we have emphasised earlier, your search for your right job must be an active, not a passive process. Some people do succeed by being reactive, not creative. They wait for vacancies to be advertised in the press, and then respond to those advertisements. Unfortunately, this traditional method of seeking employment has become steadily less effective. Press advertisements represent the 'iceberg above the water' proportion of job vacancies. Most of the vacancies are hidden from general view. You must conduct some exploration below the waterline.

We have mentioned elsewhere the importance of systematic research into the job market. There is no substitute for determined investigation allied to sound self-organisation. You will need to follow five guidelines in order to acquire and use your essential source information successfully.

Rule 1.   Find a good commercial library, or a library with a comprehensive commercial section.
Not everyone can attend the City Business Library regularly. Even those living in the Greater London area will need to balance the cost of fares incurred in visiting the City Business Library, with its unrivalled collection of reference books, against the possible disadvantage of using a more restricted local library. As a minimum requirement the library you decide to use must offer access to the following publications:-
- The quality daily newspapers – *Financial Times, Guardian, Daily Telegraph, The Independent*, and *The Times*
- The quality Sunday newspapers – *Observer, Sunday Telegraph*, and *Sunday Times*
- The quality regional newspapers – *Birmingham Post, Glasgow Herald, Liverpool Daily Post, Scotsman* and *Yorkshire Post*

(Even if you do not wish to move home remember that regional newspapers sometimes advertise jobs which are located outside their particular regional area)

- The 'quality' weekly magazines:- *Economist, New Statesman and Society* and *Spectator*
- Professional and technical journals and magazines which represent the official or quasi-official voice of a profession – for example, *Accountancy, Accountancy Age, Accountant's Record, Administrator, Airline World, Architects Journal, Banking World, Certified Accountant, Chartered Mechanical Engineer, Chartered Surveyor Weekly, Chemical Engineer, Computer Journal, Computer News, Computing, Construction Today, Drapers Record, Electrical Times, Electronics Engineer, Estates Gazette, House Builder and Developer*, and many, many others.

Benn's Media Directory, which is published annually, and should be available in your chosen library, contains detailed information on all national newspapers, regional and local newspapers, free distribution newspapers, periodicals, magazines, and directories published in the U.K., together with information on broadcasting and electronic media, and an index of the communications industry agencies and services.

Extel cards, (which are published by Extel Statistical Services Ltd.) are small and convenient to handle. They contain detailed statistics relating to turnover, profits, capital, and number of employees over recent years for quoted public companies, with a separate section dealing with unquoted companies. The current composition of the board of directors is provided, and recent and future developments are summarised. A synopsis of, or extract from, the chairman's address to the annual general meeting is often included.

We have referred previously to the *Kompass* directories which contain valuable cross references classifying companies by geographical area, economic sector, trade activity, and competitor groups. There are also *Kompass* directories for companies overseas. Consequently, if you possess a skill which is geographically transferable across national boundaries (many engineering skills, for example are marketable internationally) you might like to explore job opportunities on the continent. Work permit restrictions have been relaxed. Many British people now work in Europe, especially in Holland and Belgium where English is frequently the recognised business language in many companies.

Rule 2. Enlist the help of your library staff
Most people who decide to pursue a career as a librarian are
professional in attitude and behaviour. They are committed to the
dissemination of information and welcome requests for help and
advice. If your library does not have a particular directory or
reference book in stock, the staff will obtain a copy for you through
one of the regional lending schemes.

We know of one instance in Lancashire where a job seeker
informed the library of her job search programme, enlisted the staff
in a combined operation, and ten weeks later invited them all to a
cheese and wine celebration in the library when she received and
accepted an attractive job offer as an administration controller.

Although this particular appointment arose from her exploration
of the hidden job market, she remembered the many friendly
morning greetings and the frequent helpful questions and suggestions – "Have you seen this advertisement, Diane?" – "Could this
be a good lead for you?" – "There is an interesting job in the
Manchester Evening News today."

Most library staff also respond positively and enthusiastically to
telephone enquiries. They will usually attempt to answer a query;
extract books or magazines for you to scrutinise later when you visit
the library; and suggest reference sources if you are in doubt about
the appropriate directory or journal to peruse.

Rule 3. Initiate your own personal research
Although your library is an essential element in your job search
programme, you should also initiate some personal research as a
reinforcement. For example, you can write to, or telephone, the
head office of any public company and ask them to send you a copy
of their last annual report and accounts. There is no charge for this
service. If you live close to the company's headquarters you can
make a personal visit, and often collect an 'information pack' in
addition to the annual report.

Not all libraries file copies of company reports, hence the possible need to collect this basic information by your individual efforts.
You can often deduce from its annual report whether the company
is one for which you would like to work – and also whether there
might be a home for your skills, experience, and abilities. The
chairman's speech will usually describe the company's plans for the
future. From your standpoint a pessimistic forecast is not necessarily less promising than an optimistic forecast. No matter whether
the company is contracting or expanding, there might be a place for

you. A company in decline could need you to help in a 'turn around' programme. A company which is growing could need you to fill one of those new roles which expansion will create.

Beware of the temptation to rely on memory, and thereby approach only the 'obvious' companies. With the intense merger, acquisition, and takeover activity of recent years, many companies have changed in identity, ownership, and/or name. Other companies have diversified into new fields (which might be a fruitful source of exploration for you). This is where the professional and trade directories can be of crucial importance.

For example, one assistant shop manager known to us was interested in changing employment because her promotion was blocked by a large surplus of managers in her age group. She had worked for a national retail chain which sold books, stationery, and newspapers. Her thoughts immediately turned to major competitor companies.

On scrutinising the *Retail Directory* at her local library she realised that the DIY chains were expanding rapidly and that there were likely to be managerial vacancies in this retail growth sector. She prepared a careful 'marketing letter' to accompany her c.v., and wrote to the managing director in each of seven selected companies, emphasising the transferability of her retail expertise and skills. Four of the companies invited her for interview, and two offered her an appointment at a higher salary and level of responsibility.

The company which she eventually decided to join had been formed less than 20 years ago to specialise in the DIY market. To quote the successful applicant:- "It was not a company which came to my mind at all when I first decided to look around. I suppose I had heard about the organisation – vaguely – although I had no idea of the scope of their recent success and plans for growth. The two directors who interviewed me were so impressive that after I heard about their schemes for continued expansion I knew that I had suddenly discovered the right company for me."

In common with the *Retail Directory* many other trade directories contain details of all companies operating within a defined trade and/or sector. The information is frequently extensive and can include details of geographical locations, addresses, key executives, trade names, size, and sometimes, trading performance. We cannot overestimate the value of such directories in your job search programme. Apart from the opportunity to detect 'nonobvious', yet 'opportunity-rich' companies, you will be able to extract vital information which you can then 'recycle' when, as a prospective candidate, you forward your c.v. and covering letter to selected companies later. Thus you can strengthen your prospects of being offered interviews.

Furthermore, by 'skimming' a trade directory you will absorb the basic background to the sector and thereby provide yourself with relevant and convincing information which you can use at an interview to create a favourable impression.

When you approach a large public company for information, always contact the public relations department rather than the company secretary. In addition to forwarding the annual report and accounts the public relations department will be able to provide a wider range of material – copies of the company newspaper, news sheets, and reports to employees, for example.

The public relations department will often be pleased to add your name to the mailing list for future copies of publications, whereas the company secretary will tend to deal with an approach as a single request for a single document (invariably the annual report and accounts).

Rule 4. Keep records of your research

As your job search programme progresses you will find that one source leads to another and your research information will steadily expand in quantity – and complexity. You will quickly discover that the sheer volume of information renders personal recall an impossible task. Accordingly, you must keep records of your research in a form which facilitates prompt, convenient and accurate information retrieval.

If you are fortunate enough to possess a personal computer and are thoroughly conversant with its uses you will be able to store all your research information in your own databank and extract specific details promptly, as and when you require them.

If you do not own a personal computer you will be able to assemble an effective database by using postcard sized index packs arranged in alphabetical order. On each card you should enter the following information:-

Name of company
Address of company
Telephone number of company
Brief details of activities of company
Name of any contact executives(s)
Source of information about the company

Date when application submitted
Date of company reply
Form of company reply:–
  'Holding letter'
  Interview(s)
  Rejection letter after interview(s)
  Appointment offer letter
Your decision
Subsequent action
Brief general comments.

Your index cards can be filed conveniently in small plastic boxes, designed specifically to accommodate postcard-sized records. These boxes are available at any stationery store. Ideally, you should purchase three boxes – one to contain the 'dead' cards, as a proportion of your applications may result in eventual rejection; a second box to contain 'pending' cards representing your applications which have been deferred rather than rejected; and the third box to accommodate your recent, 'live' applications. Apart from the convenience and economy of this system, you will have access to an immediate 'visual progress report'. The sight of a large collection of both 'live' applications and 'pending' applications can sustain or improve your morale.

Rule 5.   Use your research information to review your progress
Occasionally research-oriented people derive so much satisfaction from their research activity that they begin to lose sight of the main objective. There is little virtue in research for research's sake. You need to collect relevant information which you can use efficiently to secure interviews and thereby subsequently receive job offers. In order to manage your job search programme successfully you will need to use your research information to review and monitor your progress.

If you are using postcard-sized records, a regular scrutiny of the contents of your three boxes will provide you with a quick, overall picture of your current progress – or lack of progress. At the most pessimistic level you may discover that all your letters, applications and general enquiries have produced no interviews. In that event a fundamental re-examination of your strategy is necessary immediately. There is no point in travelling down a road which is not leading to your destination. You need to plan a different route.

Again, you may find that you have won the first round of the recruitment contest by obtaining several interviews, although you may find that every interview has resulted in a rejection of your application.

You must then examine your interview technique, because you are being eliminated in the second round of each contest. If you are able to secure interviews, but not job offers, you can deduce that you have prepared a convincing c.v. and marketing letter. In some way, however, you are not reinforcing the initial favourable impression created by your written presentation with an equally convincing presence and verbal performance at interview. Concentrate, therefore, solely on polishing your interview technique.

Another possibility is that you have attended interviews without any formal decision having been reached. Typical comments after such interviews are :-

"We are just about to reorganise the sales department. As soon as we have completed the exercise we will be in touch with you again. We will certainly need two or three people with your experience."

"Our finance director is abroad at the moment. The final ratification of the appointment will have to have to await his return in three to four weeks time".

"We have had a general recruitment freeze pending a review of responsibilities. At the moment, any appointment requires a special dispensation. I will submit a case, but it may be some weeks before I can confirm an offer of the position".

Sometimes such remarks represent a supposedly polite way of saying 'Your application has been unsuccessful'. On the other hand, your informant may be stating the whole truth and nothing but the truth. There could be a valid reason for the delay. Your difficulty as a job seeker is that you cannot be sure whether such a delay constitutes a disguised rejection or an unavoidable interval before a firm offer is made. You have no option but to take each statement at its face value. Wait until the predicted reply date is passed and then, a week or ten days after that, write a polite reminder letter. Keep the letter short – but include one major point to reawaken the enthusiasm of the reader. A letter in the following style could generate a quick and favourable response:-

"Dear . . . ,

When we met on . . . (date) . . . you explained that about four weeks would elapse before you would be able to confirm the creation of a new sales position.

I am still very interested in joining your company. As you may

remember from our interview discussion, I have acquired new
accounts and expanded sales in a comparable retail sector.
    I am convinced that I could help you in your plans for
expansion.
Yours sincerely, . . . ''

At your interview the interviewer may have described company
deficiencies – or you may have detected and mentioned problems
that need to be resolved. If so, you can refer to these important
issues briefly when you write your follow up letter. You should have
summarised the key discussion points on your record cards immediately after the interview. By referring to your records, you will
be able to re-emphasise the most important point(s) – and impress
the interviewer with your powers of recall!

Your reminder letter should not include any criticism of the
recipient – or of his or her company. You may believe that the delay
in dealing with your candidacy has been unjustifiable. If so, keep
you condemnation to yourself. When you eventually join the
company you can then make constructive suggestions for the
improvement of the recruitment and selection procedures.

Summary

Five rules to follow when organising your job research programme:-
1.   Find a good commercial library, or a library with a good
    commercial section.
2.   Enlist the help of the library staff.
3.   Initiate your own personal research.
4.   Keep records of your research.
5.   Use your research information to review your progress.

11

Answer the Interviewer

Interviews vary in pattern and content depending upon the experience, personality, and preferences of the interviewer – together with your own performance and attitude at the interview. Some interviews are informal. Most interviews are conducted in a formal, or semi-formal, manner.

The general employment interview

Irrespective of the form of the interview, the general employment interview serves three main purposes:-

1. It allows the interviewer to meet you, the candidate, face to face and form some impression of how acceptable you are likely to make yourself to key staff, and to which kind of people you are likely to be able to relate. Other than seeing a videotape (in the U.S.A. candidates now use their own video tapes to supplement c.v.s) it is difficult to see how else an interviewer might make such judgements.

2. It enables the interviewer to gain some idea of 'what makes you tick' – to discover what you have enjoyed doing; what you have disliked; what you regard as your strengths; what you feel less comfortable with; what sort of people you have got on well with in the past; what sort of people you have not got on well with; and whether you are likely to be a worker or a 'floater'. From your attitudes towards other people a competent interviewer can predict the reactions and attitudes of other people towards you.

The interviewer will be assessing the source, direction and strength of your motivation to work, and your attitude to work.

3. The general employment interview permits the interviewer to check the information on your application form, to interpret it, and

to uncover new, relevant information. This is the most important aim of the interview – to obtain a comprehensive and accurate account of your past history, your strengths and weaknesses, and your successes and your failures, together with your reactions to them.

The staff agency interview

Staff agency interviews fall into a special category.

One feature which distinguishes staff selection agency interviews from others is that the interview time represents a direct monetary cost, and consequently will be strictly limited in duration. With a staff agency you are unlikely to receive a long interview. Indeed, you may be 'on your way again' in half an hour or less from the time of your arrival at the agency office.

The staff agency has four main tasks:-

To attract candidates by search or advertising.

To match jobs and candidates.

To 'sell' suitable candidates on the role to be filled.

To 'sell' to the client those candidates who can meet the demands of the role specified.

Accordingly, from a staff agency, you are unlikely to receive an unbiased view of what the job is about, or indeed, any view! Often the agency will have taken its instructions by telephone and never have met the employer. Therefore you should be careful to check with the employer direct, when you meet him or her, exactly what responsibilities, tasks, and accountabilities the job will contain and what will be the terms and conditions.

Sometimes agencies will exaggerate salaries, bonuses, holiday entitlements and other matters. Although agencies will not intend to mislead you deliberately they are likely to quote the highest salary the employer is prepared to pay. The agency will be endeavouring to present the vacancy and the employer in as attractive a light as possible. In reality the quoted salary may only be applicable to someone with much greater experience than you can offer.

What the interviewer does to identify a suitable match between jobs and candidates.

Irrespective of the duration or form of an interview, in order to match a job and a candidate successfully the interviewer will have to follow a three-step logical sequence.

First, he or she will need to produce a *job description* by carefully studying the role and determining the key tasks, responsibilities, and reporting relationships. Secondly, the interviewer will attempt to define the abilities, attributes, and experience which would be possessed by the *ideal* candidate and then translate that information into a *person specification*. Thirdly, the interviewer will be required to assess each candidate and decide how closely each candidate meets the person specification demands.

A competent and considerate interviewer should ensure that each candidate receives a copy of both the job description and the person specification. A common appreciation of the nature of the job to be filled, and a joint recognition of the ideal candidate to occupy that role, will reduce misunderstanding and confusion.

Of course, it is true that ideal candidates are seldom found. Life is rarely about perfection. As a prospective candidate you may ask the question: "Why then take all this trouble to seek the unobtainable by specifying the ideal candidate?"

The interviewer, if given the opportunity, would probably explain that there are two important reasons for this recruitment discipline. First, without a person specification there will be no objective standard against which a range of candidates can be assessed for rejection or engagement by the interviewer. Secondly, without a person specification it will be impossible to prepare training and management development plans to 'close the gap' between what the organisation needs from you, the candidate, and what you have to offer. After all, effective management is about making the best use of the available human resources, some of which will be less than perfect!

The experienced interviewer will have included a definition of essential attributes and desirable attributes within the person specification. Essential attributes are usually few in number because if you, as a candidate, are below the standard in any essential attribute, you would not normally be considered further – no matter how suitable you might be in other respects. Desirable attributes are qualities or factors which the selector would like you, as a candidate, to possess. Nevertheless if you are a little below target on one or more of the desirable attributes but are suitable in other aspects, you might well be offered the appointment in the knowledge that you could bring to the company *most* of the skills, experience and aptitudes sought.

Obviously it will be beneficial to your employment prospects if you are offered an opportunity to read a job description and a person specification prior to an interview. For example, you will then be able to study the desirable attributes, and especially the essential attributes, in the person specification and prepare yourself to reassure the interviewer when he or she begins to probe you in these crucial areas.

The interviewer's plan

Most, although not all, interviewers will adopt some form of interview plan in order to reach considered and objective assessments of candidates. The 'Seven Point Plan', originally devised for vocational guidance purposes, is used by many interviewers. This particular plan is doubly useful because it lends itself both to the specification of the ideal candidate, and also facilitates the assessment of a candidate by encouraging a selector to consider a candidate's characteristics and the job requirements under seven common factors. (It is important to study candidates and jobs in compatible terms if selection mistakes are to be avoided).

The 'Seven Point Plan' covers seven main areas:-
1.   Appearance, manner and speech.
2.   Educational opportunities and the use made of those opportunities in terms of examination passes and qualifications.
3.   Occupational opportunities and the use made of those opportunities in terms of appointments, promotion and general career progression.
4.   General intelligence and the use made of that intellectual capacity in both employment and in private life.
5.   Special aptitudes and the relationship of those skills to career and personal achievements.
6.   Disposition or temperament as expressed in attitude to, and associations with, people at work and in social groups.
7.   Special circumstances, in so far as they might affect the capacity of a candidate to fulfill the responsibilities of a role either adversely or favourably.

Although the Seven Point Plan has stood the test of time it was developed over fifty years ago and recently more sophisticated adaptations have been introduced. Of course you, as a candidate, will not necessarily be aware of the plan (if any) which the interviewer adopts when meeting you face to face. You can be sure that many interviewers will endeavour to apply their chosen interview plan in a chronological sequence. You should be prepared for this common approach.

In essence the interviewer will attempt to review, discuss and appraise your life history in chronological order. He or she will seek to cover your family background, formative years, schooling, training, any further education, interests, work history, and towards the end of the interview discuss your future plans. At each stage in the sequence your interviewer will encourage you to talk about your achievements and failures, your likes and dislikes, and your attitudes – both positive and negative.

Some interviewers reject the chronological approach because they have discovered, from experience, that too much time can be devoted to issues which are not of prime importance in relation to the vacancy. They adopt a different approach and find it more beneficial to follow the sequence of most current application forms which start with the current, or last job, and then work backwards.

This approach could be helpful to you in that you would be reviewing initially your most recent experiences. Not only are you likely to be at ease with topics which are live in your recent memory, but they will be items which you will have expected to be raised. Thus you should have already prepared your considered responses and, if so, will be able to get the interview off to a good start. Thereby you will generate some initial self-confidence which should reduce apprehension and strain for the later stages of the interview when you might be moving into unknown territory.

Your interviewer will determine his or her own interviewing method. As a candidate you must be prepared for any approach. If you are asked to start with your early history you must be careful not to bore the interviewer. Move fairly rapidly through this topic unless invited to elaborate on any points.

The interviewer will already have read your application letter, or application form (if one exists), although if have been 'head-hunted' you may be expected to produce a career history later. Where you have submitted documentation you can assume the interviewer will have read it although he or she will welcome a verbal summary, especially if you emphasise your achievements and successes.

How the interview is likely to be conducted – and traps for you to avoid

A good interviewer will maintain a friendly, sympathetic attitude at all times. He or she will not appear shocked at anything you may say, nor appear to criticise, even indirectly. Some interviewers will use sympathy as a kind of absorbent to extract from you opinions, beliefs, and attitudes that might be better concealed from your point of view. For example, beware of the temptation to expose strong criticism of your last employer. The more friendly the interviewer the more essential that you endeavour to keep topics under your control and, as far as possible, that you reveal only what will be to your advantage. Keep any hard luck stories to yourself.

One executive we counselled said he had come for assistance because he felt that his personality was too strong and put off the people who interviewed him. We agreed to see him, and set him in front of a tape recorder to analyse how he dealt with the question "Tell me about your career to date." His reply took about ten minutes – the first mistake – but more damaging was his presentation of his work history. His personality certainly was forceful, but at the level of job he was applying for seemed quite appropriate. What was getting him rejections, however, was not his personality but what he was saying about his previous employers. When we played back the tape he saw the point immediately. One firm was incompetent; the managing director of another was cheating the Inland Revenue; another had totally wrongly assessed the market for a new product, and so on.

His assessment of them all was probably quite accurate – but interviewers do not want to hear someone running down all previous employers. We told him to go and write down all the good things he could say about each previous company he had worked for, and then come back for a second session.

He duly returned with a quite different approach and version of his previous experiences, and went back to the task of finding another job. He had got nowhere during the previous four months, but three weeks later we heard he had been offered and accepted just the kind of job he had hoped for, and that he attributed it to his changed interview performance.

The questioning techniques of interviewers

Competent interviewers use 'open-ended' questions, which you cannot answer by a 'Yes' or 'No' reply, or a one-word answer. The object is to encourage you to talk freely about things the interviewer wants to hear about. After all, the more you say, the more information will be available when the interviewer makes his or her final judgements. An opening gambit adopted by many interviewers is to start by saying "Tell me about yourself".

Watch that you do not fall into the trap of becoming subservient and agreeing with the interviewer too easily. Many interviewers pose 'leading' questions that suggest the preferred answer. Beware of questions such as those that begin with the interviewer saying "I suppose you . . . " or "No doubt you thought that . . . " Do not agree with the interviewer out of politeness, or a willingness to please, if the interviewer has got it wrong.

If you are faced with a complex question such as a question and a supplementary in the same breath, you may be uncertain of what is being asked, or you may need time to think of your response. If so, ask the interviewer to rephrase the question.

The deadliest questions are often the simplest, and/or the vaguest, because you have no idea how the interviewer wants them answered. You do not know what to leave out, nor what to include. You may be led to volunteer a lot of information that you might never have given had the question been more specific at the outset. For example, "Tell me about the things which matter to you" is a vague but searching question that an interviewer might use to unearth information about your attitudes, convictions, standards and opinions generally. The interviewer might continue with – "That is very interesting. Go on . . . "

Sometimes the interviewer will not follow up questions with other questions. By just grunting and nodding in an encouraging fashion he or she will expect to elicit more information. By repeating the last word or words which you have just spoken, the interviewer can also 'trigger off' your further responses and reactions. For example, you might say " . . . and then I had a disagreement over policy". The interviewer could repeat "policy?" in an enquiring tone, expecting you to start talking again and thereby provide him or her with yet more information.

Thus the sophisticated interviewer will be hoping to collect a lot of information from you by questions that seem somewhat vague; by making encouraging noises; and by repeating the last words that you say. By adopting such a 'laid back' approach, inevitably the interviewer will make it more difficult for you to stick to a prepared line unless you have previously rehearsed thoroughly the responses which you will make to possible questions – and follow-up questions. On the assumption that you wish to maximise your chances of being offered a job, you will have no choice but to adapt to whatever style the interviewer imposes on the interview. The lesson to be drawn is not that it is pointless in preparing for the unpredictable, but rather that your preparation must be that much more thorough.

The interviewer will try to probe areas where you have not succeeded; activities, relationships and situations which you have disliked; and any embarrassing experiences which you have suffered. Therefore expect this investigation and be prepared. You are certain to be asked about your attitudes. "What did you enjoy about that job?" "What else did you enjoy?" "How did you find the general conditions?" "Tell me some of the things you did not enjoy?" "How did you find the people you worked with?" "What help did you get from your colleagues?" "Did you ever have reason to complain about anything?" "How did you feel when you were disciplined?" "What are you looking for in a change of job?" "What would be particularly important for you?" "What is your idea of an ideal employer?" The possible questions are endless.

You will also be asked about your skills. "What are you considered good at?" "What do you do best?" "What are you not so good at?" "Tell me some of the things you are proud of." "What would you say are your strengths?" ". . . and weaknesses?" "How were your abilities utilised?"

The interviewer may also enquire about your leisure activities. He or she will do so for two reasons. First, your leisure and recreational pursuits could provide the interviewer with a guide to your aptitude for leadership and/or cooperation in conditions where progress will be dependent upon the use of interpersonal skills, rather than on the exercise of formal authority. Secondly, your private 'spare-time' activities could be an indication of the level of your motivation and drive. People who have well developed activities in their spare time often carry over similar attitudes and energies into their work; whereas those are inclined to drift aimlessly often lack motivation at work.

Consequently the interviewer may not just be content to leave it that you collect stamps in your spare time. He or she may attempt to find out how many stamps you own, whether your collection is specialised, its value, how often you study it, add to it, show it, what satisfactions you derive from it, and what are your future plans for the collection. Avoid the unnecessary risk of claiming something as an interest just because you think it will look appropriate on the application form or letter. You may be asked in some depth about any interests which you have indicated. You could show up badly as a result if your knowledge and involvement are found to be superficial and your responses to the interviewer betray your lack of real commitment.

Finally, the interviewer may ask if you have any questions of your own. Raise one or two sensible questions, preferably about matters of policy rather than about trivialities like "how long is the lunch break?" For example, ask about training, or how your work will be assessed, or what book the interviewer might recommend for you to read so that you can brief yourself on the firm or industry before the next meeting.

Anticipating your interviewer's interview plan

In order to be successful in any form of negotiation you must acquire some understanding of the tactics and strategy likely to be employed by your adversary. You can regard your job interviews as important negotiations which you hope to win. It could be beneficial for you to consider the framework of the interview plan which most trained interviewers are likely to adopt when they meet you.

Here is an example, which, allowing for minor adaptations, represents a standard interview plan:-

Twelve essential steps for the interviewer

1. Plan the interview. Time? Location? Duration of interview? Seating arrangements? Privacy? No interruptions? Candidate's expenses? Read application form again. Prepare check-list.
2. Welcome the candidate. Introduce yourself. Establish rapport by adopting a friendly approach. Ensure that the physical needs of the candidate are satisfied. Help the candidate to relax.
3. Explain the selection procedure. Likely duration of the interview? Any other selectors to be met? Visits to be made? Next stage of process? Decision date?
4. Provide additional information about the job. Explain key tasks, responsibilities, and reporting relationships. Concentrate upon areas of the job description which might require further elaboration. Invite questions.
5. Begin the interview by asking nondirective, open-ended questions. Start informally, but (after mentioning your intention to the candidate) take limited notes. Encourage the candidate to provide

general information by questions such as: "Would you like to tell me something about your background? Your education? What did you do after school? Just a broad outline . . . "

6. *Guide the candidate into a definition of ambitions and aspirations.* Ascertain how the candidate would like his or her career to develop. What does he or she find attractive about the job on offer?

7. *Discover attitudes.* What is the attitude of the candidate to work in general and the role in particular? What are the likes and dislikes of the candidate?

8. *Identify skills and special aptitudes.* "What were you good at?" "Where do you see your strengths and weaknesses?" "Tell me about some of your achievements."

9. *Review leisure activities.* Leisure activities can be revealing in terms of aptitudes, skills, interests, initiative, leadership qualities, managerial ability, and social flexibility.

10. *Assess personality.* Encourage the candidate to project his or her personality into the discussion. Whilst personal matters should not be raised too early in the interview, the personality of the candidate is an important factor in the selection process. It is vital to assess the preferred management style of the candidate in both favourable and unfavourable conditions.

11. *Check factual information and invite questions and comment.* The application form should contain a range of factual information. During the interview, areas of uncertainty may have emerged. Check points of doubt. Invite questions – including comment on the interview itself.

12. *Wind up effectively.* Consult your check list. Check on practical points – expenses, the return journey. Try to see the candidate out yourself. Explain the next step. Finally, write a report.

Not every interviewer will have benefited from formal training in interviewing techniques. There are still selectors who regard the interview as an opportunity to exercise personal prejudices. We have encountered interviewers who would not recruit short men, underweight women, men dressed in green clothes, men and women with red hair, men wearing suede shoes, women with a preference for colourful spectacle frames and men and women with a limp handshake.

Although you cannot hope to counter such idiosyncratic views you should be assured that many interviewers, especially those in large companies, will be following an interview plan similar to the one outlined above. If you are familiar with the structure of an interview plan you can tactfully fill in the gaps if your interviewer forgets to cover a particular area or topic. For example: "You have covered my career thoroughly. Are you going to ask me about my other skills – my languages for example?" "Do you want to raise the question of references?" "Will you be outlining the next stage in the selection procedure?"

After the interview is over *

After the interview is over the interviewer will be trying to form a mental picture of you. He or she will be considering questions such as: "Can I see that candidate doing this task in this company?" "How will that candidate adapt to our own staff and our own working environment?" "Will that candidate have the motivation and determination to succeed in the job which we have to offer?" By posing such questions the interviewer will begin to compare your background, experience, skills, qualifications and personality with the demands of the job description and person specification.

What your interviewer will have endeavoured to record

Most experienced interviewers construct an 'interview check list and assessment' form which they find convenient to use. The major factors to be assessed will be common to all forms, although the actual terms used will vary. 'Energy' might be called 'drive' or 'motivation' defined as 'application'.

Here is an example of such a form:

Candidate: .... Interviewer: .... Date:..........

INTERVIEW CHECK LIST AND ASSESSMENT   **RATING
(encircle)

**RATINGS: 5=excellent, 4=good, 3=adequate, 2=poor, 1=unsuitable

Impact and physique What immediate impact does he/   5 4 3 2 1
     she make by virtue of appearance, manner, speech
     and hygiene? Are there any features about this per-
     son which would bar him/her from consideration?

Education and skill Does he/she meet the basic require-   5   4   3   2   1
ments? Are there any weaknesses? Are there
strengths that could be developed? Does he/she have
the potential to go further?

Brains and abilities How intelligent is this applicant? Is   5   4   3   2   1
he/she a quick learner? Does he/she possess any
special abilities? What is the evidence?

Motivation Will he/she stick at the job, and work hard to   5   4   3   2   1
become successful? What is the evidence? e.g. What
use has been made of opportunities so far – in
education, work, spare time? Does he/she become
deeply involved?

Work History and Attainments Has he/she made steady   5   4   3   2   1
progress so far? Does he/she possess any special
knowledge in the area we require?

Stability Is this applicant's work record a steady one?   5   4   3   2   1
Has he/she a record of regular attendance? Did he/
she like former colleagues? Does he/she criticise past
employers destructively? Does he/she have a 'chip
on the shoulder'? Is he/she self-reliant?

Work Attitudes Why is the applicant interested in this   5   4   3   2   1
job? What is important to him/her in physical or
social surroundings? What has he/she found out
about this job so far? Why has he/she left previous
jobs? Does he/she want more status? money? interest? prospects? to learn more? How will this job
satisfy these aims?

Personality Note his/her strong points, but are there any   5   4   3   2   1
features about him/her that would make him/her a
doubtful applicant? e.g. too shy, outspoken, academic, aggressive, unfriendly, inflexible?

Summary What are this applicant's strong points? What   5   4   3   2   1
are the weak points? Is he/she, on balance, a reason-
able applicant for this job – who would be more
likely to succeed than fail?

Decision Offer, see again, refer to another interviewer,   5   4   3   2   1
short-list, reject, or other? Specify what action will
be taken next.

Typical interviewers' questions

Here are some typical interview questions for you to consider. Where appropriate you can rehearse your replies. Obviously we are not recommending that you prepare a series of word-perfect, stilted replies to all these questions. Nevertheless, they are all questions which are frequently asked. Some time spent considering your best response, in principle, could prove invaluable when you reach the interview stage. Your friend or counsellor could read them to you, one at a time, and then comment on how convincing your replies sound. If your counsellor considers any of your replies unimpressive, try answering them again in a different way until your response does carry conviction.

Let us begin by talking about your experience so far. Tell me about your present job.

What exactly do you do?

I am still not clear about the scope of this job. Give me some idea of a typical day, starting with your arrival at the office/factory/shop.

How did you happen to choose this job?

How has your job turned out?

What do you like about your job? . . . What else do you like about it?

What aspects are you good at? . . . What else are you good at?

What aspects of the job are difficult? . . . How do you cope with them?

What are the people like whom you work with?

Tell me about your boss.

Why are you interested in a possible change?

What are you seeking in your next job?

Have you tried to make a change in your own company?

What aspects of a job are important to you? . . . What other aspects . . . ?

How will you make a judgement about your next possible employer?

How will your present company react if they discover you want a change?

What do you think they would say about your performance if asked?

When did you last have time off for sickness? . . . And the time before that?

What were the key problems you had to solve?

Tell me about your *previous* job (or the previous jobs)

Tell me about your life outside work.

What do the other members of your family do for a living?

Have you discussed your plans with them?

What activities do you take part in outside work?

How do you spend your free time?

How would you prefer to spend your time generally if money were no barrier?

When in your life so far have you had to be most independent?

What sort of people do you get on with best?

What sort of people do you not get on so well with?

Have you run across any difficult people at work? . . . Give an example.

Give another example.

What plans do you have for your future?

What might attract you about this job? . . . What else attracts you?

What do you think the important features would be in your ideal job?

What would be the critical requirements, in your opinion, to do that job successfully?

How do you measure up to them?

How successful do you think you have been so far? . . . Why do you say that?

Now tell me something about your early life, your education for instance?

What did you enjoy at school? . . . Why?

What did you not enjoy? . . . Why?

What would you say were your strong points in relation to employment?

What are your not so strong points?

How would you describe your own personality?

Are there any others in your family? . . . In what ways are you like him, her, them?

In what ways do you differ from him, her, them?

Are there any other questions you would have liked to have been asked?

What questions would you now like to ask me?

Pet questions

The above list should have given you a good idea of the kinds of questions which you may be asked. Ideally you should be prepared to answer any or all of them. Unfortunately for you as a candidate, not all interviewers follow the same pattern. Some interviewers use pet questions because they believe that unusual questions will stretch the candidate. For example, "If you were loaned a million pounds for one year at a 12% rate of interest, what would you do with it?"

Such questions are impossible for you to predict and therefore you will not be able to prepare for these surprises. If you are confronted with a question which is strange and unusual, then you will have to do your best. If you really cannot think of anything reasonable to say in reply, explain that you find it a very difficult question. With such questions you prefer to take your time over them and give a considered reply, rather than make superficial comments. You may be lucky, and the interviewer may not press you further.

An important warning – ensure that you do not contradict any of your written statements

Many candidates fall into the trap of contradicting written statements, made in a c.v. or covering letter, by verbal comments during an interview. They do so for three main reasons:-

First, they forget what they wrote in their c.v. and covering letter. We all suffer from lapses of memory. Unfortunately, if your mind suddenly goes blank during an interview, you may be tempted to guess – possibly with disastrous results. The interviewer will compare your verbal answer with your written statement, note a significant discrepancy, and may assume that you are dishonest.

Secondly, they may become nervous or slightly confused during an interview. Under a largely self-imposed mental strain, some candidates deviate substantially from a written statement in a fallacious attempt to make a convincing case. In practice they almost inevitably suffer the reverse effect because their personal integrity is then called into question. You must resist any temptation to engage in sudden flights of fancy and/or impulsive exaggerations.

The safest method of self-protection from these risks is to read a copy of your c.v. and covering letter carefully at least twice before each interview, in order to memorise all key dates, career details, and important personal facts. Then take copies of the documents with you to the interview so that you can benefit from a last minute 'reminder' before you conceal the papers in your pocket, handbag or briefcase.

Thirdly, candidates may be too anxious to please the interviewer. There is a strong tendency to agree with leading questions in order to create a favourable impression. Unfortunately, you may be tempted to endorse an assumption which contradicts one of your written statements, or to agree with a statement which is unfavourable to you.

Summary

Ten tips to remember when preparing yourself for an interview:-

Prior to the interview
1. Be ready for an informal, semi-formal or formal interview.
2. Expect leading questions.
3. Prepare and rehearse yourself for leading questions.
4. Obtain a job description and person specification, if possible.
5. Review yourself in relation to the job description and person specification if possible.

At the interview
6. Do not behave aggressively.
7. Do not condemn your previous employers.
8. Do not become subservient.
9. Ensure that you do not contradict statements in your c.v. or covering letter.
10. Think about the interviewer's own interview plan.

12

Prepare for Interviews

When you arrive at the stage of being invited for interview you may feel that the battle is nearly won. Not so: it is only the beginning of the contest.

When asked to give a report on their progess, some job seekers will say something like this: "I'm doing quite well. I have had 12 interviews and been short-listed three times." They have not appreciated that there is no point in being short-listed if you are not the candidate who is offered the job – apart from the benefit of the interview practice. In job seeking there are no prizes for coming second or third. What you have to do is to maximise your chances of coming first. In this chapter we give you some hints of how to succeed.

Brief yourself on the company

The first thing to do when invited for an interview is to brief yourself thoroughly about the company. If you have not already done so, consult Extel cards. Note down all the key statistics, like volume of sales or turnover for the past three or four years, and profits before tax. Also look at any extracts from the chairman's most recent annual report or speech at the annual general meeting, or press release.

Do not be deterred if the company appears to be going backwards or facing hard times. A poor trading position may be one of the reasons why they need *you*. It may be an opportunity for you to demonstrate your worth. Hoewever, it does help for you to be aware of the situation before you go for the interview. During the interview, whilst you are being asked questions, indicate that you have investigated the company's recent history and do know something about the current or most recently reported trading position.

If the interview is scheduled for a week or two ahead you will have time to telephone or write to the company secretary, state that you are scheduled to have a business meeting with the company in the near future, and request a copy of the annual report and accounts. This will give you further information which you may be able to turn to your advantage.

Arrive for the interview early – and prepared

Arrive for the interview at least 15 minutes early. Visit the lavatory in order to wash the newsprint off your hands if you have been reading a newspaper on the way. Adjust your dress or straighten your tie. Fix your hair. Brush dandruff or dust from your clothes. Perhaps even give your shoes a wipe. We know an executive who always carried a highly polished pair of shoes in his brief case and would put them on before being interviewed. This may seem obsessional, but it is important to look your best.

Not only must you look clean and tidy, and have eliminated any body odour problems, but you must also dress appropriately. There is no rigid formula to follow. Try to learn from your first one or two interviews what the norm is likely to be in the kind of company to which you have applied. Sometimes that will mean dressing differently according to the type of position within the firm you are visiting. For example, if you are a woman applying for a creative job in an advertising agency, the norm may be trainer shoes, a sweater, and jeans. If you appear in a dark formal suit you may be viewed with suspicion. However, the same agency might expect to see you in a dark, formal suit if you are applying for a job as an account executive.

Wearing a beard may burden men with an unnecessary impediment. Beards take a long time to grow, and their owners are often very possessive about them. As a job seeker you should recognise that some interviewers are prejudiced against beards, feeling there is some defect that the beard is concealing, or that it is a sign of dangerous nonconformist tendencies. If a beard is not the norm in your target companies, then, if you want to cut down the time you will take to get another job, shave it off. Once you are safely on board the company, you can grow it again, if you wish, in all its splendour!

When you arrive early for your interview you will often be able to study copies of company magazines provided in the reception area. These will offer yet more information about the company you are visiting. Take a quick look through all that you see and note any interesting facts. If you can make reference to them in the interview it will demonstrate that you are alert and interested in their company and its activities. Do not worry if there is no such information available, because none of the other candidates is likely to be in a better position than you.

Adopt a friendly approach

If it is possible, and appropriate, to make a little small talk with the receptionist, and perhaps with a secretary who escorts you to the interview, then do so. Avoid brusque or pompous comments. You may not think it can affect your prosects of success, but a secretary or receptionist is often asked by the interviewer for an impression of you. Although a good report might only marginally enhance your chances, an adverse comment, even from this quarter, could be damning.

Be pleasant and affable. Bearing in mind that people enjoy talking about themselves, ask a few questions like "How long have you been in the company?" "Have you had a holiday yet this year?" or "How do you find the journey travelling to and from work?"

When you first meet the interviewer, smile. Make certain you have his or her name correctly, and at appropriate points during the interview and at its conclusion, use it. People like hearing the sound of their own name and could be pleased that you have remembered it.

Do not sit down until you are invited to do so. On no account smoke, even if it is indicated that you may do so if you wish. The interviewer may not be a smoker. He or she may have asked you if you wish to smoke out of courtesy, or to help you relax, but may not enjoy the experience if you do so.

Many interviewers tend to make their mind up about candidates early in the interview. Research has shown that interview judgements are generally made within the first four minutes. Although your interview may go on much longer than that, your interviewer may only be looking for evidence to justify a decision already made intuitively.

The first question will often be an open-ended one, which you cannot answer by 'Yes' or 'No, or by another one-word answer. It may take the form of "Tell me about yourself". Your reply must be one which you have prepared previously. For many candidates who have not rehearsed the answer, this opening question can be a killer.

Open with a rehearsed statement

The secret is to have decided, in advance, what points you want to get across in your opening statement, and to limit your reply to no more than two minues. Even better if you take only a minute and a half! People who carry on longer than this can be viewed as egotistical and boring. Although professional selectors are trained to talk only 20% of the time and listen for 80% of the time, many of the interviewers you will meet are unlikely to have had any training in interviewing. They prefer listening 20% of the time and talking for 80% of the time. You must give them the opportunity to do what they enjoy and will make them feel good about the interview. Consequently, faced with a question like "Tell me about yourself" talk for two minutes at most, then stop, and ask "Are there any other points you would like me to cover, or to elaborate on?"

This gives the interviewer the chance to talk, which he or she will welcome, and perhaps to focus on areas of particular interest, some of which you will already have led him or her to think about.

When we say that an opening statement should be rehearsed, we do mean just that. We recommend that you practise replying to the "Tell me abut yourself" question in front of a sympathetic, intelligent listener armed with a watch, so that you can get some useful feedback. Rehearse until you and your counsellor are satisfied that you can put across all the points you wish to stress in a maximum of two minutes.

The content of what you wish to say may be broadly similar from interview to interview. Yet if you know a few facts about the particular company, and the approximate nature of the job, you can indicate in your opening statement how your interests, skills or experience might fit the company's requirements. Do not be presumptuous and tell your interviewer what he or she should be looking for. You could be wrong! But you could make one or two general statements like:-

"One thing I would bring to this job is a very disciplined

approach to the buying function." or "If appointed, I should be able to bring a good deal of up-to-date knowledge about the use of integrated spread sheets" . . . or whatever.

Part of the interview is likely to consist of your being asked to run through your career to date and expand the details you have already given in your career history or application form. This will require you to talk about companies where you have previously worked, and what you have done, how you progressed, and why you left. On no account criticise the companies or the executives who worked for them, or in any way give the impression that you are a resentful or embittered person. Not only does it create a very bad impression but you do not know whether the people you criticise may be known by, or even friends of, the interviewer.

Again, make certain you are fully briefed on your own career history by referring back, prior to the interview, to your achievement statements used to prepare your c.v. Express your success and degree of effort or level of responsibility in concrete terms. For example "I was in charge of a department of 14, three of whom were graduates and two had professional qualifications". or "I managed to improve the unit cost of hiring clerical workers by 60%."

If you do not tell the interviewer what you have achieved in your various roles, he may not think to ask you, and you will have lost an opportunity to promote your case.

There are a number of questions which you can almost guarantee will be asked by one interviewer or another. You should have thought about these in advance and rehearsed your answers. (Again, in front of a friend or counsellor) A list of these questions is provided in chapter 11.

The most important ones are:
Why do you wish to join us?
What could you bring to the job?
Why did you leave, or wish to leave, your previous company?
What would they say about you if asked?
What are your strong points and weak points?
What salary are you seeking?

Some interviewers will go further and set the candidate hypothetical problems to solve.

Body language

Be careful about your body language and posture. Your posture and movements will be dictated to some extent by the chair in which you are invited to sit. If you have a choice, pick an upright chair rather than an armchair. You will look far more businesslike sitting on the former. Whilst appearing confident and relaxed is a desirable attribute, it is possible to overdo it and to seem casual. Do not sit with your hands in your pockets, play with pens or spectacles, or fiddle with your handbag.

Questions that need rehearsal

The question "Tell me about yourself" can either be one of the most difficult to answer or one that you can use to make a strong favourable impact, according to how you have planned your response.

As you have prepared yourself for this question, you should be able to give a successful two-minute (maximum) summary of your skills and strengths, highlighting how these might benefit your prospective employer. You should have predetermined and practised at least four or five key points you would like to put across.

Interviews with those employers or consultants who have placed a job advertisement to which you have replied are relatively straightforward. The more difficult interviews are those where the consultant or company have called you in 'on spec' out of general interest. Then you will not have prior information about the possible job, or range of jobs, for which you are being interviewed, or for which you could make yourself appear eligible. Early in the interview you should try to obtain information by some judicious and diplomatic probing. For example: "Before I deal with that topic, perhaps I could be even more helpful. If you could tell me a little about the kind of opportunities there might be in this company my replies could be more relevant."

Such an opening reply on your part demonstrates a degree of assertiveness, a logical outlook, a preference for thinking before you speak, initiative, and a certain shrewdness – all qualities which will give you a better score. Of course, the interviewer may decline to be drawn, but you will not have lost anything by trying.

Ask your own questions

At the conclusion of the interview be ready to ask the interviewer some questions of your own. You could preface these by indicating that you already know something about the company, such as: "I have seen the most recent annual report and accounts, so I have some feel for the turnover, profits, capital employed and recent trends. However, I should like to know about . . .

- the split between various market segments . . .
- whether your customer base is shifting in respect of (age, socio-economic level) . . .
- how you hope your customer profile will have changed, if at all, over the next five years.
- the company's attitude to damaging the environment, social responsibility etc.

Interviewers do not, as a rule, like 'puddings' – people who are uncommunicative. You will enhance your own rating by asking intelligent and appropriate questions.

When you are invited to attend for a second interview there may be one or several different people you have not previously met. Do not hesitate to ask some of the same or similar questions that you raised before, even if you feel you know all the answers by now. Candidates have lost potential offers of employment after the second interview – often the one which counts – because they did not probe and ask questions. The new interviewers thought that the candidates lacked initiative and motivation, whereas the candidates had grilled the selectors at the first interview, had received all the answers, and saw no reason to ask them again.

Furthermore, you may get slightly different answers from another interviewer and you can then ask how the different view-point arises.

You may feel that this amounts to some kind of subterfuge on your part. Remember that interview judgements are very fallible and you do not want to be passed over for the wrong reasons. Besides, getting a job is much harder than carrying it off. Once you are inside an organisation there will be people to help you. If you are sufficiently senior you will be able to pick your own team or brief your own external consultants.

Summarise

As the interview comes to a close it is worth while leaving the interviewer with a summary of your own impressions of where matters rest. Do not take more than a minute, but recap on some of the points you decided at the outset you would make. For example: "May I just sum up our discussion? The company is one that interests me and it seems to me that my experience and track record of . . . operating to tight timetables/controlling costs/developing sales of £1m in the first year/producing error-free returns over a long period . . ." (or whatever you have previously decided will be a selling point) " . . . could make a strong contribution."

If you feel the style suits you, end with what one counsellor has described as the most effective seven words you can utter, "If appointed, I won't let you down!"

Write a follow-up letter

You have not yet finished with this interview. After returning home write to the interviewer thanking him or her for seeing you, and reiterating your enthusiasm for the company and the job you discussed. Few of your fellow applicants will have thought about following up their interview in this way. If the selector is interviewing a dozen candidates for the job he or she will have forgotten quite a lot about the earlier candidates by the time the last one is interviewed. You are more likely to be remembered if the interviewer has been prompted to think about you for a second time by a pleasant letter.

Do not close down other opportunities yet

No matter what favourable impressions of your likely success you take away from the interview, do not slack off in your job search. Even if you are assured that an offer will be forthcoming and you would like to accept it, do not abandon your campaign to obtain other interviews. Maintain your positive attitude. A lot of factors can intervene between someone's promising to make you a job offer and that offer being typed, signed and posted.

Even after an offer has been made it could still be withdrawn. One personnel executive was invited to meet the chairman of a major PLC after accepting an offer of employment from the managing director and having handed in his notice to his current employer. He wished to review some of the terms and conditions which had not been determined – car, private mileage, pension scheme, life cover, BUPA and foreign travel arrangements. After the personnel executive had raised the first three items on the list, the chairman said to him: "I don't employ quibblers. The offer is withdrawn."

It is also possible to find yourself declared redundant during the period between accepting an offer and starting employment with the new company, for a variety of reasons – the unexpected sale of the company; a takeover battle which imposes a freeze on recruitment; a management buy out; the death or resignation of the key executive; the loss of an important contract; government intervention; site closure; or other twists of fate. It is essential not to sign off with other companies who may be interested in you until you are certain that you have been offered a job, have accepted that job, and have received a formal letter of appointment which constitutes a contract of employment. If that contract is subject to the receipt of satisfactory references, ensure that the references have been supplied and found acceptable before you abandon your job search elsewhere.

Summary

Ten rules for dealing with your interviewer
1. Brief yourself on the company.
2. Arrive for the interview early – and prepared.
3. Adopt a friendly manner.
4. Open with a short rehearsed statement.
5. Be careful about your body language.
6. Use your rehearsed answers to the interviewer's stock questions.
7. Put your own rehearsed questions to the interviewer.
8. Summarise at the end of the interview.
9. Write a prompt follow-up letter.
10. Do not abandon your job search until you are certain about a job offer.

13

Tackle the Tests

You may be invited to complete a test or tests during a selection procedure. Theoretically you will be able to exercise the right of refusal. In practice, if you want the job under consideration, you will be well advised to cast yourself in the role of a willing volunteer! Accordingly it could be helpful if we explain briefly the purpose and construction of tests. You could find that a little knowledge removes any apprehension, increases your self-confidence, and thereby improves your performance when you take the tests.

Tests can be classified into three broad categories:-

1. Intelligence tests

Intelligence tests consist of carefully devised problems presented in a standard way, so that one candidate's competence can be compared with another's. Before tests are introduced into regular use they are given to many people so that the 'spread' of scores can be determined for the kinds of occupations in question.

Undoubtedly there is some hostility on the part of candidates to the use of intelligence tests in selection. Much of this suspicion stems from ignorance. Sometimes critics say that we lack any definition of intelligence which is acceptable to the majority of psychologists: but the same can be said of electricity, which we can measure, and use, without being able to define its precise nature!

One definition of intelligence is 'all-round thinking capacity' or 'general mental ability'. Most selectors will agree that intelligence in this sense is important in selection. All selectors hope to be able to determine the level of intelligence of candidates, but research has demonstrated that it cannot be estimated accurately in an interview. The only way to assess the level of intelligence accurately is to measure it using tests. The important question is not 'Do I believe in intelligence tests?' but 'Is there a better way of measuring it?'

Intelligence tests can be used in many ways in selection. A selector is not obliged to appoint the most intelligent candidate. By relating intelligence to achievement the selector can obtain an indication of the candidate's drive, application, and energy – and motivation is a vital factor in job success.

After the administration of tests the selector may find that two candidates with the same qualifications and similar backgrounds have significantly different levels of intelligence: one much higher than the other. The lower-scoring candidate could be a 'high' achiever and may have done better at school, college, or in work than anyone could reasonably have expected given his or her level of intellectual endowment. The same level of achievement by the superior intellect would not be as impressive. A comparison of a person's achievement in relation to level of intelligence can be an accurate guide to his or her level of motivation. The professional selector can only obtain this kind of information from a study of test results.

If you are asked to complete an intelligence test it could be a timed test or an untimed test. The timed tests are designed so that they cannot normally be completed in the allocated period. Obviously, if every candidate could answer all the questions correctly within the specified time limit, that information would be of little value in making comparisons. Your ability to secure more correct answers than your competitors before the time runs out is what will interest the selector.

Untimed tests, often known as 'Power Tests', are constructed so that the questions are presented in an ascending order of difficulty to reach a near insoluble level. For most people there will come a saturation point in answering the questions beyond which they will be unable to progress. In selection procedures untimed tests are seldom used because of the practical problems in administering them. Determined and/or obsessive candidates have been known to sit for hours in an attempt to answer every question correctly! Any intelligence test you are asked to complete will almost certainly be a timed test. As a consequence you must manage your time efficiently in order to achieve the best possible results. Remember to :-

- Read the instructions carefully before you commence the test. Usually the test admistrator will go over these with you.
- Take full advantage of any practice examples and practice time which you are given.
- Ask questions before you start the test if you are uncertain of the procedure to be followed.
- Avoid wasting time on any question where the answer does not become obvious quickly. Carry on to the next item. (You will be unlikely to be able to finish all the items, so concentrate on those you find you can do.)

2. Personality tests

The use of personality tests has been popular in America and in continental countries for many years. In Britain they have been used more sparingly, although they have been in more common use during the eighties. These tests aim to measure personality factors rather than abilities, and to predict whether a candidate is likely to adapt to a particular work group easily. They can indicate personality trends which might otherwise be concealed, and in particular, some main dimensions of personality can be assessed. Tendencies to be introverted or extraverted can be detected; and so can tendencies to be stable and adjusted, as opposed to being emotional and affected by feelings; or to be radical or conservative.

The selector will be trying to make predictions about the candidate's likely social behaviour, and his or her value system. Unless a candidate is willing to cooperate and provide accurate and unrestricted information about himself or herself, the task of personality assessment becomes very difficult, if not impossible.

Obviously, intelligence tests have right or wrong answers. Practice and foreknowledge of what to expect improve your score by a factor of around ten per cent or so. This is one reason why all intelligence tests start with a few unscored examples. It might therefore be useful for you to read one or two paperback books which give you practice examples (such as *Know your own IQ*) and thereby prepare you to deal more confidently with any intelligence test with which you may be confronted.

Personality tests differ from intelligence tests in that there are no right or wrong answers. You are usually asked a number of different possible responses to each question and asked to express a preference for one rather than another. You may answer 'honestly' or 'dishonestly' but there are 'honest' or 'dishonest' answers and some tests have a lie-detector scale incorporated in them so that any inconsistencies will be revealed.

If you are presented with a personality test you should try to answer truthfully or give the answer which is normally most appropriate for you. This is for two reasons. First, if you attempt to give the answers which, in your opinion, the interviewer would prefer, you may make some incorrect assumptions. Secondly, it could be in your own interests to reveal 'your true self' because ideally there should be a match or balance between your personality, abilities and experience, and the demands of the job under consideration. If there is a serious mismatch you might nevertheless be able to undertake the work successfully – although at considerable personal cost in terms of psychological stress and physical strain.

One technician known to us obtained a job as a production manager. As he explained: "I needed a higher salary for domestic reasons, so I applied for several jobs. When I was asked to complete some personality tests I could see what my answers should be in order to match the profile. The company wanted someone who was pushy and bossy."

"I gave the answers which the company wanted, and backed them with statements during the interview which were really out of character for me. Since then I have had to close a department, make staff redundant, and act in a manner which is altogether too ruthless for me. I am not sleeping well, and have been short-tempered with my wife and children. I would rather return to the research environment of a technical development department. Money is not everything, especially when you feel under constant pressure."

Because there are no apparent 'correct' or 'incorrect' answers to personality test questions it is often easy to misinterpret the instructions. Recently we invited a highly authoritarian manager to complete a personality questionnaire in order to assess his management style. There were four possible responses to each situation posed, and these had each to be placed in preferred order, number 4 for the response which most closely represented his likely reaction, number 3 for his next preferred response, then number 2, and finally number 1 for his least preferred response, the one he was most unlikely to make in practice.

Our manager, who was strongly 'action-orientated', completed the questionnaire without reading the instructions, or listening closely to the explanation, and assumed that 'No. 1' should be his first choice. As a consequence his preferred management style emerged as a 'retiring, research-inclined diffident attitude' – exactly the opposite of his controlling, impulsive, confident behaviour. A careless test administrator might not have picked that up, and the candidate might have been wrongly assessed accordingly.

We suggest that when you are invited to complete personality tests you should:-

- Read the instructions thoroughly before you commence answering the questionnaire.
- Resist the temptation to look for the 'best answers'.
- Give honest replies to all questions.

3. Aptitude tests

As we have seen, intelligence tests attempt to measure general mental ability. Personality tests attempt to answer the question "What *sort* of person is this?"

Aptitude tests are designed to assess an individual's potential for acquiring and developing certain specific skills (for example, computer programming or flying an aircraft) from the results derived from specially constructed test 'batteries' – groups of tests constructed and assembled for this specific purpose.

It is in the interests of an employer to determine the capacity of a potential recruit to absorb training (which could be expensive – in the case of an airline pilot, for example, about £100,000, and for an RAF pilot about five times that) before offering an appointment. It is pointless, for both parties, to start an individual on an extended training programme when the prospects of completing it successfully, as predicted by aptitude tests, are minimal.

Thus an employer and a prospective candidate share a common purpose in the successful determination of individual aptitude for a category of jobs which are dependent on the acquisition of a specific skill. Research has demonstrated that, for example, some unsuccessful dental students failed to qualify because they were deficient in manual dexterity – not because their written answers in examinations were unsatisfactory. The unnecessary waste of time and acute personal disappointment suffered by such students might have been avoided by the judicious use of aptitude tests.

You are unlikely to be invited to complete aptitude tests unless you are seeking a highly specialised job where a particular skill is of particular importance, you do not possess it already, and you would have to be trained to acquire it. For example, if an airline is recruiting trained pilots from other airlines it does not use aptitude tests, but actual tests of flying skill administered in a flight simulator and in real flying.

Your responses to aptitude tests cannot be faked or disguised. If you are required to take aptitude tests, for whatever reason, our advice would be:-

- Consider the results of any feedback carefully and in general accept the conclusions and recommendations.

Of course, if you are a really determined person you can partially overcome a lack of aptitude for acquiring a skill by extraordinary persistence. Your success will depend on the skill in question and the level of performance you hope to attain. It would be profitless for you to try to become an artist or an architect, for example, if you have no artistic sense. On the other hand it is possible that many applicants who fail, say, the British Airways aptitude tests for pilot training, might nevertheless still be able to learn to pilot an aircraft, although perhaps not to the standard of flying skills that the airline requires for its jet planes.

With all three categories of tests you will often receive some feed back from the test administrator, and if you do not it is legitimate to ask for it. Ethically anyone requesting you to complete a test should outline the purpose of that test and subsequently discuss your performance with you.

Summary

Seven tips for tackling tests:-
1. Read the instructions thoroughly before you commence the test.
2. Utilise fully any practice time which you are allowed.
3. Ask the test administrator questions to remove any doubts before you commence the test.
4. When taking a timed test avoid wasting time on any question where the answer is not obvious quickly.
5. Answer personality tests honestly.
6. Accept the conclusions of any aptitude tests, at least as far as that company is concerned.
7. Request feed back from the the administrator concerning the purpose of the test and your performance. Such further self-knowledge could be useful to you.

14

Negotiate

What is the best possible deal?

There is no single formula which we can recommend to help you to negotiate the best possible pay package once you have reached the stage of discussing a firm job offer. What constitutes 'the best possible offer' will depend upon one, or a combination of several, of eight factors:

- Your own attitude to money
- Your own bargaining strength – or weakness
- Your own peferences and aspirations
- Your own dislikes and aversions
- Your own motivation
- Your own negotiating ability
- The manipulative and/or persuasive skills of your prospective employer
- Luck

By definition every job represents a distinct decision which is made in relation to a unique person. Although we cannot provide all-purpose guidelines which will guarantee the best deal for all, we do offer some general observations about each of the eight factors which might be helpful.

Your own attitude to money

Herzberg and other research sociologists have suggested that there is a basic level beyond which money ceases to be the prime, or even an important, motivating factor in a person's career decisions. Everyone needs food, clothing, and shelter. Money must be found to purchase the basic essentials in life. Beyond that point priorities change as leisure, family, work satisfaction and personal freedom become relatively more important.

Whilst the theory is sound in principle, it is inevitably interpreted differently in individual cases. 'Basic essentials' can mean anything from food, clothes and modest shelter to dining at expensive restaurants, wearing designer dresses or Savile Row suits, and owning both a town house and a country cottage. Under the influence of sophisticated national sales and marketing campaigns, together with a widespread anxiety to 'keep up with the Joneses', the luxuries and extravagances of yesterday have been transformed into the indispensables of today. As a consequence, many people experience a constant need to earn more – and often anticipate increased earnings by steadily extending their credit commitments. Others enjoy acquiring wealth for reasons of social status, security, or individual satisfaction, rather than to facilitate personal consumption. Many wealthy people restrict their expenditure on individual luxuries and adopt a surprisingly modest life style.

If you happen to be one of the minority who 'pursue money for money's own sake' then obviously the level of remuneration will be your sole motivating force in any pay negotiation. For the majority of people, who do not necessarily sell themselves to the highest bidder, a combination of factors will determine the optimum negotiating objective or objectives.

Your own bargaining strength – or weakness

If you are 57, lack formal qualifications, possess no scarce skill to sell, and have been unemployed for over a year, you should accept any reasonable offer without quibble. Often minor problems or disadvantages can be solved or rectified once you are working for a company and performing well. Furthermore, you will find it easier to secure another job if you are in employment.

On the other hand, if you are 32, graduated with an honours degree in computer sciences, speak French, and have had significant experience in both technical development and marketing, you are likely to be pestered by approaches from head-hunters. You can afford to adopt a 'take it or leave it' attitude. One such person known to us decided to end a telephone conversation with an executive search consultant by saying "I am not really interested. Tell the company that if they want me they will have to double my salary." The company did, and four months later she joined her new employers at a salary which even she regarded as extravagant.

'Playing hard to get' can sometimes prove highly lucrative – provided that you start from a strong bargaining position, or that you are thought by your interviwer to hold all the aces (even though you do not).

Your own preferences and aspirations

For some people job satisfaction, scope for initiative, and individual freedom at work constitute stronger influences than pay. "The money is good but the job is not worth the hassle" represents a cry from the heart which is not unknown among commuters in south-eastern England as they sit in traffic jams or travel in crowded trains.

Surprisingly, many prospective candidates who are not mainly 'money-motivated' fail to bring the factors which concern them into negotiation. Few such candidates even attempt to negotiate a more acceptable job description, for example. Flexitime, job sharing, working partly or wholly from home, study leave, self-employed status, sabbaticals, reporting relationships and extended leave are a few of the issues which could be introduced into the negotiation discussions by a prospective candidate. If any of these or other factors are important to you, raise them at an appropriate stage. You might be surprised at the extent of your success – especially as some of the 'concessions' would cost the employer little or nothing. You could also win bonus points for creativity and initiative.

Your own dislikes and aversions

Some people have much stronger convictions than others and tend to react strongly against those who conflict with or appear to threaten their beliefs. For example, men and women with a firm commitment to civil liberties and racial equality will condemn apartheid in South Africa. Members of Friends of the Earth and Greenpeace will oppose the discharge of poisons from industrial processes that pollute rivers and seas. Some fervent animal lovers campaign against the fur trade.

Sometimes people with a crusading spirit join organisations with which their attitudes are not entirely compatible in the belief that they may be able to reform them from within. Such efforts are almost certainly doomed to failure. If you are a 'campaigner' with strong feelings about certain issues it would be unwise to involve them in negotiation, and you should be wary of accepting employment with any organisation whose intrinsic activities conflict by nature with your beliefs. Your campaigning energies might perhaps be more usefully directed through the appropriate pressure group.

If, however, you are one of those who think that 'a job is a job, and it does not greatly matter what business we are in', you are unlikely to be troubled by moralistic issues.

Your own motivation
There is not doubt that strong personal motivation can enable you to surmount even the most formidable obstacles. The much-quoted maxim "If at first you don't succeed, try, try, try again" is golden advice for job seekers. Strong motivation will help you to obtain interviews and eventually the job you seek – and motivation, allied to negotiating skills, will enable you to obtain the best possible deal for yourself. Interviewers tend to be impressed by candidates who seem self-assured, show confidence in their abilities, and do not undersell themselves.

Your own negotiating ability
Even in the most bureaucratic organisations personnel managers and other executives usually have some room for manoeuvre when discussing remuneration with a prospective candidate. In normal circumstances the interviewer will wish to fill a vacancy and will be inclined to 'stretch' (within limits) in order to conclude an agreement with a person who seems competent and available. The art of negotiation is not to overplay your hand by making unreasonable demands which drive your interviewer into a corner. The inevitable rejection of an extravagant claim may result in the subsequent rejection of you as a candidate!

You must avoid equally the risk of 'selling yourself short' unnecessarily. There is every reason for the unemployed person with limited or no bargaining power to accept any reasonable offer gratefully. For those in more fortunate circumstances, however, there is usually scope for extracting marginal improvements.

As a general rule, do not take the initiative in pay negotiations. As far as possible delay the 'crunch point' until you are convinced that there is no doubt in the mind of the interviewer that you have become the person to whom that interviewer is determined to make a firm and acceptable job offer.

The manipulative and/or persuasive skills of your prospective employer
In one retail company we know there was one particular personnel officer who was always used whenever difficult and/or unattractive vacancies arose. As one of his colleagues explained, "Nigel could sell central heating in the Sahara. He makes people think that it is a

privilege to come and work for the company irrespective of the job. Nigel can fill even the most protracted vacancies once he turns on the charm. Candidates never seem to query the pay or the conditions."

You may be confronted by a 'smooth talker' who disguises the unpleasant aspects of a job and concentrates on the 'selling points'. When you recognise that that is happening you should probe the grey areas and extract what negative information you can that your interviewer may be reluctant to volunteer. For example, if a role has been filled by a number of people in rapid succession, questions about the reasons for transfer or resignation could be revealing.

Luck

Luck will not be a reliable aid in your job search – or in your pay negotiations. Nevertheless it can sometimes play a significant part, however unpredictably.

Luck may come your way but it is no acceptable substitute for self-motivation and personal performance in your job-search programme.

Remember that a job offer can be withdrawn

A verbal offer of a job which is accepted verbally constitutes a valid offer of employment – although such an offer might be difficult to substantiate in the courts if a dispute should ensue. In the words of Groucho Marx, "A verbal agreement is not worth the paper it is written on." But a verbal offer is normally quickly followed by a written offer, which constitutes formidable evidence of a legal agreement once a written acceptance of the offer has been delivered.

If an offer is satisfactory but complex, accept in principle immediately – but request time to consider the detail

You are unlikely to receive a complex offer of employment. Only a minority of companies adopt unusual policies and practices. Some organisations apply the 'cafeteria approach' whereby you are given choice in selecting from a wide range of elements which form the total remuneration package. The company makes a commitment to finance a package worth a specified sum and leaves you to determine the balance between your preferred fringe benefits and the basic pay. You might need time to calculate the value to you of individual benefits before you can decide on the optimum formula. You should accept such an offer promptly if you regard it as satisfactory in general, and resolve the details later.

When you have accepted an offer (and started work) write to thank all contacts
Successful job seekers sometimes overlook the moral obligation to thank contacts. You may have written to or telephoned friends, consultants, personnel executives, employers, and a range of other people, some of whom may have taken considerable trouble to help you either directly or indirectly. You should thank them all in writing or in person. After all, you may need their help in the future. And do not forget, when you are safely ensconced in your shiny new job, that they or others may one day need your help in the way that you needed theirs: put it back into the kitty!

Summary

Ten rules to help you in negotiating a good deal:
1. If your bargaining position is weak, do not quibble.
2. Play 'hard to get' only if you start from a position of strength.
3. Negotiate a more acceptable job description if you are motivated mainly by non-financial considerations.
4. Do not convince yourself that you can change the attitudes of a company whose main activities are in conflict with your ethical principles.
5. Remember that motivation, allied to negotiating skill, will secure the best deal.
6. Develop your negotiating abilities. Do not take the initiative in talking about money – sell yourself before discussing the price.
7. Beware of the persuasive interviewer with an unattractive job to sell.
8. Research the hidden costs of accepting a job – especially if you will be expected to move home.
9. Remember that a job offer can be withdrawn.
10. If an offer is complex but satisfactory, accept immediately in principle but request time to consider details.

15

Deal with Consultants

Professional personnel executives and consultants who are engaged in recruitment should always operate within the framework of a ten-point code of ethics, established by the Institute of Personnel Management. As a job-seeker you should be aware of the following simple but comprehensive code of recruitment ethics:-

1. Job advertisements should relate to real jobs.
2. A job description and a person specification should be supplied to short-listed candidates (and ideally to all candidates).
3. Job advertisements should normally reveal the identity of the company.
4. Job advertisements should indicate the action to be taken by prospective candidates.
5. All applications should be acknowledged.
6. All applicants should be informed of the progress of the selection procedure.
7. Illegal discrimination should be avoided.
8. Unethical discrimination should be avoided.
9. All applications should be treated as confidential,and detailed personal information should not be sought unless it is relevant to the selection process.
10. The prior approval of candidates should be obtained before references are requested.

The code is voluntary, and unfortunately unethical breaches are common. For example, a minority of consultants have been known to advertise fictitious vacancies in order to acquire an impressive stock of c.v.s for their databank.

Breachs of the code of practice are not confined to the lower levels of recruitment. Indeed, some of the worst misdemeanours occur when top appointments are made. "The more important the appointment, the more haphazard and questionable is the selection procedure" has been a complaint ventilated repeatedly at conferences of the Institute of Personnel Mangement. As observers have indicated, apprentices are usually selected thoroughly. Aptitude tests; school reports; parent/employer discussions; and multiple interviews are common place in apprentice selection. Yet directors join main boards by processes that are shrouded in mystery.

Job descriptions and person specifications are often scarce commodities for senior executives. Furthermore, the involvement of personnel departments (within which a body of selection expertise might be expected to reside) frequently peters out towards the top of the management hierarchy. At the higher levels, personnel specialists are often superseded by executive search consultants. As we have explained earlier, the vast majority of senior vacancies are not advertised. They are handled by 'head-hunters' who, by definition, operate in secrecy and are reluctant to volunteer information about their practices.

As a consequence, independent and reliable research into the 'head-hunting' profession is limited. Nevertheless it has been demonstrated that a majority of 'head-hunters' in a respresentative sample survey had received no formal training in interviewing techniques and selection validation. A majority had a background in sales and marketing before becoming search consultants. Only 9% had worked previously in a personnel-related role. More than half the 'head-hunters' had received a public school education and attached great importance to social acceptability when considering candidates for their short-lists.

One prominent search consultant emphasised to us: "I aim to submit a short list of at least three candidates, all of whom will interview well when they meet the client company. In consequence I concentrate on identifying people whom the directors will like."

You will almost certainly be invited to meet a head-hunter if you are seeking a senior executive or equivalent appointment. Information about search consultants is limited and difficult to obtain. Nevertheless, as a starting point you should read the appropriate entry in the *Executive Grapevine*, the directory of executive recruitment consultants, which is edited by Robert Baird and should be available in your library. Although many of the consultancies provide the minimum of information, you will be able to extract several items which you can use to stimulate discussion at your interivew.

You will need to make a good impression at that interview, even though the consultant would not be your employer if you were to be offered the job. You have two hurdles to clear. First you must persuade the consultant that you are worthy of inclusion on his or her short list for submission to the client company. Secondly, only then will you have the opportunity to convince the client company, at a later stage, that you are the candidate who should be offered the appointment.

When you meet a head-hunter to discuss a specific job you should adopt the following five point plan:-

1. *Request copies of the job description and person specification, if you have not already been supplied with them.*

Ideally, you should have received copies of the job description and person specification by post. In that event, you should study both documents carefully before meeting the search consultant.

2. *Raise questions on both the job description and the person specification with the search consultant.*

Obviously, if you have received the documents in advance you will have had an opportunity to prepare – and rehearse – some considered questions; but you may be handed a job description and person specification during an interview discussion. Beware of the temptation to make quick, impulsive comments. Request a short interlude in order to read the paper and/or ask your interviewer to summarise briefly the main points in both documents.

3. *Establish the identity of the client company.*

Frequently, search consultants will withhold the identity of the client company until you attend for interview with them. There is usually no justification for preserving secrecy beyond that stage. When you have submitted a c.v., met a consultant, and been prepared to answer a number of probing questions, it is not unreasonable to expect to be given comprehensive information in return.

Be on your guard if you are unable to establish the identity of the client company – especially if you have not been supplied with copies of the job description and person specification. A combination of excessive secrecy allied to scanty information can be a signal that you may have been enticed into an exploratory and personally revealing interview on the basis of a nonexistent job. There is nothing wrong in going to see a consultant for an exploratory chat with no specific job in view. In fact, we would recommend that. After all, the more people you get to know, and who know that you are in the job market, the better. But it should be on an open basis, and the purpose of the interview should have been revealed to you in advance.

4. *Take brief notes.*

Although you may have been provided with copies of both the job description and the person specification, you may find that the information they contain is inadequate. As many selection consultants have not benefited from professional training it is not surprising that their written documents are sometimes sketchy and imprecise. You should attempt to fill the gaps by raising questions and taking notes.

It is important to record the gaps, omissions, and areas of uncertainty. Once you have passed the first test and ensured your inclusion on the final shortlist, you will be interviewed by one or more executives from the client company. They will be fully conversant with the vacancy to be filled and will probably have formed a clear picture of the ideal person to be sought. At this second stage you are likely to be faced with comments and questions such as "No doubt you have received a comprehensive description of the job and a detailed person specification from our consultants . . . " or "I expect that we can take it for granted that you know all there is to know about the job and what sort of person we are seeking." This will be the time for you to produce your notes and say, if true, something along the following lines: "As a matter of fact, there are some doubts in my mind. I raised several important questions at the first interview to which I was unable to obtain complete answers. Perhaps we could run through these points briefly . . . "

By adopting this approach you are likely to be perceived by the interviewer as a systematic, enquiring, businesslike person. On the other hand, if you are tempted to agree with the client interviewer's initial implication that you did receive a full briefing from the consultant, your lack of detailed knowledge will subseqeuntly become apparent during the ensuing discussion. If you then attempt to justify your ignorance by saying "Unfortunately, the consultant did not go into the job description in detail, and the briefing was rather vague . . . " you may be regarded as having shown insufficient initiative in not having asked appropriate questions, or perceived as a 'wriggler', or at worst, somewhat dishonest.

Furthermore, your notes from your first interview with the consultant should enable you to prepare and rehearse some crisp questions for the crucial second interview with the client. Executives are usually impressed by articulate candidates who pose relevant and demanding questions. One managing director has quoted Professor Revans, saying that " ' Top management is about asking questions, not any questions, but the right questions'. When appointing my managers and executives, I always prefer those candidates who pose sensible and searching questions."

5. *Concentrate on your prime objective – inclusion on the final shortlist.*

There is a danger of confusing your objectives in relation to your two interviews. Obviously when you meet the company representatives your aim will be to obtain a job offer. At the first interview with the consultant, however, your task is different. You must persuade the consultant to submit you as a short-listed candidate to the client company. To succeed in this aim you cannot afford to antagonise the consultant – and you need to convince the consultant that you will behave as a credible candidate if short-listed. Accordingly you must not embarrass the consultant by exposing his or her limitations and inadequacies, nor must you give any indication that you might do so to his or her employer, the client, at the second interview.

You may be confronted by an incompetent consultant who lacks the expertise to analyse a role, isolate the key tasks, and define the desirable and essential personal attributes to be sought in the ideal candidate. Alternatively it could be a very specialised or technical appointment which only those engaged in that particular line of work would have a hope of being fully conversant with. Consultants tend to be asked by companies to do all their recruitment for them at particular levels, regardless of whether it be for a genetics scientist, a general manger of a subsidiary, or financial director of a fish farm.

Remember that the consultant has been appointed to handle an assignment which could represent an attractive recruitment opportunity for you. By all means ask questions about the role, but if you find that the consultant cannot supply answers, abandon that line of enquiry. A consultant who is made to feel inadequate may regard you as too abrasive. After all, you will be able to make a note of the unanawered questions and raise them later with the company's representative in a productive and constructive way.

You must demonstrate that you will prove a good ambassador for the consultant before he or she will short-list you. Although the consultant cannot ensure that you will be offered the appointment, he or she has the power to prevent you from being considered any further.

Most 'head-hunters' stress the importance of 'getting the chemistry right' between candidate and employer. A typical consultant explained to us: "I look for people who will do themselves credit when they meet my clients. Thereby I can rely on profiting from the reflected glory. I am not interested in people who are overassertive, and rock the boat at interviews. I would reject the most brilliant person if that candidate did not know how to behave at an interview."

In practice you might discover that a company would prefer an outstanding candidate who was unorthodox in several respects. The chief executive of one leisure company said to us: "I am not interested in grey, conformist candidates. I look for competent people whom the company really needs – not for people whom everyone will like. For me, selection is not some form of popularity context." It is worth remembering the opinions of that chief executive if and when a search consultant refuses to include you on a shortlist, although you fully understand the demands of that job, and genuinely believe you could succeed. You can 'go over the head' of the head-hunter and write directly to the company executive responsible for the appointment. Of course, the search consultant will not welcome this intitative on your part. Do not worry – you have nothing to lose!

The head-hunter will probably refuse to consider you for any further assignments, but there are hundreds of consultants. They do not operate an all embracing 'hit list', or industry-wide 'proscribed list', and the loss of one consultant from your contact register will not suddenly render you unemployable. We are aware of several instances where job-seekers have decided to ignore an initial rejection by a consultant and succeeded in obtaining interviews with the client companies direct. In two cases out of nine the job seeker was offered and accepted the appointment, a 22% success rate which compares favourably with success rates by more orthodox methods!

Although we do not to wish to give the impression that many recruitment consultants practise illegal or unethical discrimination, research by organisations such as E.P.O.C. (the Equal Pay and Opportunites Campaign) has demonstrated that unfair discrimination is more widespread than commonly supposed. The malpractice is more prevalent with search consultants than with recruitment consultants who normally advertise vacancies in the press. One leading search consultant explained to us that the success of his business " . . . was built on the ability to provide our clients with the discrimination they seek – discreetly. Some of our clients do not like women, Catholics, Jews, coloured, the Irish, the disabled, or people over 50. Because we are not obliged to advertise vacancies we can satisfy our clients by screening out any unacceptable candidates without those candidates being aware of what is really happening."

Of course, by definition, all selection must be an act of discrimination – unless dice are used. The appointment of one candidate inevitably necessitates the rejection of other candidates. The question is not whether discrimination is practised, but rather what type of discrimination is applied. In the following paragraphs we briefly review some of the forms of discrimination which you might encounter and, where possible, suggest appropriate methods to combat unethical or illegal discrimination.

Age discrimination
Age discrimination is prevalent in the UK, as a scrutiny of advertisements appearing in the press will confirm. Considerable talent is wasted or underused because of an irrational preoccupation with age. In many countries, including Canada, Finland, France, Israel, Mexico, and the U.S.A., age discrimination is illegal. As yet there are no signs that the UK intends to follow the international lead and outlaw age discrimination here. You may be surpised to learn that the older person has a better chance of a final interview through the 'head-hunter' route than by press response in the U.K. British 'head-hunters' have not applied such a punitive policy towards the over 50s as many personnel executives and press-orientated consultants have displayed.

Frankly, there is not much you can do to combat age discrimination where it is deeply ingrained. For the reasons we have mentioned earlier, you should not misrepresent your date of birth.

If you are an older person and after rational discussion have failed to convince a consultant or company interviewer that an arbitrary age limit should not be imposed, then direct your job search elsewhere. Fortunately there are enough selectors about who will judge you on your competence rather than on your age. Furthermore, as we have already explained, by exploring the hidden job market you will be able to obtain interviews with companies which use an age limit as one method of controlling the number of applicants they have to deal with arising from press advertisements. Frequently such companies are willing to appoint an older, competent person who makes an individual, speculative approach.

Disability discrimination

Employment protection for the disabled and handicapped in Britain has never been strong. Consequently, unemployment among the disabled and handicapped has risen disproportionately, notwithstanding conclusive research evidence that the work performance of such employees tends to be significantly better than the average work performance by those who are not handicapped.

Our advice to anyone who is suffering from a disability is – do not reveal the information unless you are compelled to do so. Interviewers who would not knowingly invite a disabled person for interview will sometimes be prepared to offer the same person a job if the disability only becomes apparent at the interview stage, by which time the applicant will have had a chance to make a favourable impression.

Race discrimination

Unlike age discrimination, and disability discrimination, which may be unethical but not illegal, race discrimination *is* illegal. Notwithstanding the efforts of monitoring bodies, such as the Equal Opportunities Commission, race discrimination persists. The Institute of Personnel Management's joint standing committee on discrimination on several occasions has declared that " . . . there is still widespread evidence of racial disadvantage, both in obtaining jobs and in promotion prospects . . . " Clearly, you cannot change your race in order to overcome prejudice. Furthermore, you may not wish to follow the advice of some people and change your name if it happens to identify you as a member of a particular racial group. As a general rule, if you do encounter race discrimination you should enlist the help of the Equal Opportunites Commission or one of the specialist advisory bodies. Although you may not be eventually successful in securing the job, you could obtain compensation after taking your case to an industrial tribunal and/or the courts.

Discrimination by religion

Religious discrimination is more common in certain areas of the UK than others – particularly Northern Ireland, Merseyside, Clydeside, and the City of London. The discrimination can be applied in 'both directions.' One City company excludes Jews from the boardroom . A competitor welcomes Jews in such top jobs. A major retailer dislikes Catholics in senior executive roles. Another retailer prefers Catholics as executives. Although such 'compensating prejudice' may balance statistically, there could be geographical distortions as is the case, for example, for Catholics in Belfast. Much as we deplore discrimination on religious grounds, there is little effective legal remedy for you to contemplate.

Sex discrimination

It has been said that sex discrimination legislation in the U.K. has been one of the causes of the growth of 'head-hunting' – in order to circumvent the law. Clearly you do have legal redress – whether you are a man or a woman – if you have suffered discrimination on the grounds of your sex. Of the many successful actions pursued, a considerable proportion relate to discrimination in the pre-interview stage. In other words, the prospective candidate was denied the opportunity of real consideration solely or predominantly on the gender basis. Sometimes any latent prejudice can be overcome – provided that an interview is allowed to take place.

If you are confronted by sex prejudice which you cannot overcome by rational discussion your eventual redress (as with race discrimination) can only be legal action. Initially you should approach the Equal Opportunities Commission, who will be able to provide you with advice, support, and legal aid (when necessary) at no cost to you.

All recruiters, whether they be personnel executives, consultants advertising in the press, or 'head-hunters' should be operating in accordance with their professional code. Discrimination by ability should be the selection criterion.

Summary

Eight tips for dealing with consultants
1. Request copies of the job description and person specification.
2. Raise questions on the job description and person specification.
3. Establish the identity of the client company.
4. Take brief notes.
5. Concentrate on your prime objective, inclusion in the short list.
6. Do not antagonise the consultant by emphasising his or her deficiencies.
7. Endeavour to encourage 'selection by ability'.
8. Take action if you suffer illegal discrimination.

16

Bibliography

We do not suggest that you should read all or any of these books, but if they are available in your chosen library you may like to look at those that seem relevant to your needs.

Benson, E. *A guide to redundancy law* Macmillan 1985

Bolles, R.N. *What Colour is Your Parachute?* U.K. edition, Ten Speed Press 1983

Booth, A.L. *Stressmanship*. Severn House 1975

Burows, Giles *Redundancy Counselling For Managers* Institute of Personnel Management 1987

Carnegie, D. *How to Win Friends and Influence People* Kingswood Press 1987

Clutterbuck, D. *Everyone needs a mentor* Institute of Personnel Management 1985

Courtis, J. *Interviews - Skills and Strategy* Institute of Personnel Management 1988

Eysenck, H.J. *Check your own IQ* Penguin

Eysenck, J. *Know your own IQ* Penguin

Handy, C. *Understanding Organisation* Penguin 1985

Heald, T. *Networks* Coronet 1985

Higham, M. *The ABC of Interviewing* Institute of Personnel Mangement

Nathan, R. and Syrett, M. *How to Survive Unemployment* Institute of Personnel Management 1981

Stewart, A. and Stewart, V. *Tomorrow's managers today: the identification and development of management potential* Institute of Personnel Management 1981

Suter, E. *Contracts at Work* Institute of Personnel Management 1982

American publications that may be obtainable in the U.K. or from your library

Half, Robert *The Way to Get Hired in Today's Job Market* Bantam Books 1983 ISBN 0-533-23374-2

Irish, Richard K. *Go Hire Yourself an Employer* Anchor Books 1978 ISBN 0-385-13638-2

Jackson, Tom *Guerilla Tactics in the Job Market* Bantam Books 1981 ISBN 0-553-20599-4

Morin, W.J. and Cabrera, J.C. *Parting Company - how to survive the loss of a job and find another successfully* Harcourt Brace Jovanovich ISBN 0-15-671046-3 (pbk)

Payne, Richard A. *How to Get a Better Job Quicker* Taplinger Publishing Company ISBN 0-8008-3964-1

Directories

Extel cards
Kompass
The Executive Grapevine Baird, Robert B.
The Personnel Manager's Yearbook AP Information Services Limited.